*The thing that hath been, it is that
which shall be; and that which is done
is that which shall be done: and there
is no new thing under the sun.
— Ecclesiastes 1:9*

The Power of the Tabouret Principle:

Bible-Inspired Strategies to Build a Sustainable Business, Career, and Ministry

Alex Marchuk

advisory agency
THE TABOURET PRINCIPLE

Contents

Abstract

We often hear that the Bible has practical applications. However, those who make this claim usually focus on using Biblical truths to regulate behavior and relationships between people. But is it possible to apply Biblical principles more broadly — for example, in business, career, or ministry? Are there practical Biblical truths that can help organize a business, career, or ministry in a way that brings the desired results, maintains a balance between personal and professional life, and ultimately influences the world for the better?

As I approach writing this book, I bring with me experience from working in large Fortune 500 international corporations, where I built my career from Sales Representative to General Manager. I also have experience as a co-founder and manager of regional, national, and international companies.

WHO WILL BENEFIT FROM THIS BOOK:

- Church leaders and ministers who want to develop a growth strategy for their community or ministry.

- Christian entrepreneurs and business owners seeking to combine Christian values with effective management and expansion.

- Managers and executives facing challenges in managing people, motivating teams, and resolving conflicts.

- Professionals who want to improve their skills while adhering to Christian ethics.

- Startups and young entrepreneurs starting their business or ministry journey and seeking support in building a strategy and finding resources.

- Nonprofit leaders and foundation managers aiming to attract more resources, optimize processes, and ensure the sustainability of their ministry.

In this book, I often reference definitions from Wikipedia or dictionaries because I've seen how people sometimes spend too much time and effort trying to prove their point — only to realize that they had different interpretations of basic terms.

Each chapter includes practical examples and exercises designed to help you better understand and reinforce the material. After all, as the saying goes: "Hear it — forget it, see it — remember it, do it — understand it!"

FOOD FOR THOUGHT

Most of you probably remember this verse from the Bible:

So faith comes from hearing, and hearing through the word of Christ.
— Romans 10:17

If faith comes from hearing, does that mean the saying is wrong? How can faith come from something people tend to forget? In fact, if you think about it, you'll see there's truth in the saying!

A believer who drifts away from the Lord usually stops reading the Bible, prays less, and surrounds themselves with people who have nothing to do with faith. They stop sharing revelations from the Word and discussing life situations from a Biblical perspective. For faith to grow strong, one must constantly hear the Word of God — read it, pray over it, reflect on it, listen to others, share insights, and engage in conversation about it.

It's no coincidence that one of God's instructions to Joshua was this:

This Book of the Law shall not depart from your mouth, but you shall meditate on it day and night, so that you may be careful to do according to all that is written in it. For then you will make your way prosperous, and then you will have good success.
— Joshua 1:8

The more we surround ourselves with God's Word — hearing it, speaking it, reflecting on it — the wiser and more successful our decisions will be! That's why it's important to fill your life with the Word of God. In today's world, we are bombarded with information every day. To resist the influence of external ideas and emotions, we must intentionally create time to immerse ourselves in God's Word for guidance, encouragement, and comfort. The more we engage with God's Word, the stronger our passion, wisdom, and desire to follow the will and commandments of our Heavenly Father will be.

We should also focus on the practical application of Biblical truths. The saying highlights that true understanding comes only through action. The New Testament reinforces this idea:

For as the body apart from the spirit is dead, so also faith apart from works is dead.
— James 2:26

To keep your faith alive, you must put it into practice! Living out your faith is the best way to spread the Gospel. Our actions and decisions have a greater impact on those around us than our words ever could. This is how Jesus lived — He fed and healed those who came to Him. And this is how we should live too:

Let your light shine before others, so that they may see your good works and give glory to your Father who is in heaven."
— Matthew 5:16

Therefore, it's important not just to read the text but to take notes, highlight ideas that resonate with you, discuss them with your peers, colleagues or close ones, complete the practical exercises, and apply the insights to your projects. This is how you will gain the most benefit from this material — and create something that truly can change the world for the better!

Acknowledgments

First and foremost, I thank the Lord for life and salvation! For the Word of God, which holds an endless depth of wisdom and provides everything we need for life!

I am grateful to my family and close friends for your constant support and encouragement — I have always felt it!

I thank the leaders I had the privilege of working with. Your example, ideas, and passion continue to inspire me!

Introduction:
The Tabouret Principle

What has been will be again, what has been done will be done
again; there is nothing new under the sun.
— Ecclesiastes 1:9

Do you know that, according to statistics, out of 100% of small and medium-sized enterprises (SMEs) opened in Ukraine within a year, about 50–60% close down within the next year; another 20–30% close during the second year. Additionally, 10–15% close in the third year. This means that only about 10% of businesses celebrate their third anniversary!

FOOD FOR THOUGHT

United States: Data from the U.S. Bureau of Labor Statistics (BLS) shows that approximately 20% of new businesses fail within the first two years after opening, 45% within the first five years, and 65% within the first 10 years.

United Kingdom: The Telegraph reported that 60% of new businesses fail within three years, and 20% go bankrupt within the first year. Similarly, the Office for National Statistics shows that only about 40% of new businesses are still operating after five years (2014–2019).

Italy: The National Institute of Statistics states that between 80% and 90% of businesses close within the first two years.

Why does this matter? Because behind every statistic are real people — with their lives, hopes, and expectations. Of course, some businesses are intentionally created as short-term projects, designed to fulfill a specific goal and then close. But the majority start with big plans, commitments, and dreams. For these founders, closing their business — essentially facing bankruptcy — can feel like a personal and professional collapse. It can strain relationships, cause financial ruin, and, in some cases, lead to devastating personal decisions.

Yet, some companies have endured the test of time. I've had the privilege of working for a few of them.

One such example is the American company Kraft Jacobs Suchard (now Mondelez International), a recognized leader in chocolate (brands like Milka, Toblerone), coffee (Jacobs, Carte Noire) and snacks (Lux and Estrella potato chips). This company was founded in 1825 — almost 200 years ago!

Another long-standing company I had the opportunity to work for is Colgate-Palmolive, a leader in oral care products (Colgate toothpaste and brushes), as well as body care (Palmolive, Mennen, Lady Speed Stick). William Colgate started selling scented soap in 1806 and later introduced flavored dental cream (toothpaste). In 2006, while working for the company, we celebrated the 200th anniversary of the Colgate brand!

FOOD FOR THOUGHT:

The oldest known company still operating today is the Japanese company Nishiyama Onsen Keiunkan, which has been running a hotel business since **705 AD.** Remarkably, the company has been managed by **52 generations** of the founding family.

It was during my career in international corporations that I experienced a personal encounter with God, repented, and became His child. While observing business decisions firsthand, I began to wonder: What makes these successful companies different from SMEs? Why do they grow and thrive while others struggle and fail?

At the same time, I was attending Bible school and studying Scripture on my own. I began to notice how many business management principles — like hiring and selection, motivation, financial management, marketing, and sales — align closely with Biblical principles. And then it struck me...

The oldest "project" — estimated to be between 5,785 and several billion years old — is Life on Earth. What's astonishing is how meticulously designed and resilient it is! Despite human actions that harm both themselves and the planet, life persists. Every morning, as we open our eyes and take that first breath, countless processes are happening within us and around us: billions of cells in our bodies die and are reborn; the Earth continues its orbit around the Sun, and the Solar System moves through the universe; day follows night, seasons change, and the water cycle continues...

So what's the difference between building a business or ministry and sustaining life on Earth? Are there underlying principles or laws that support the success of God's creation — principles that could be applied to create a long-lasting, successful business or ministry?

The answer is YES, and I want to share those insights with you in the following chapters of this book. But first, let me explain where the Tabouret comes in.

In the context of this book, the Tabouret is a metaphor designed to help us better understand and remember the principles of successfully building projects based on Biblical truths.

Metaphor — a figure of speech in which a word or phrase literally denoting one kind of object or idea is used in place of another to suggest a likeness or analogy between them (as in drowning in money).

A tabouret is a simple chair with three legs and a seat without back or arms, for one person:

What is the value of this metaphor?

Firstly, for a tabouret to be stable, it only needs three legs! According to basic geometric axioms (i.e., things that don't need proof), if there are three points (three legs), they define a plane, in other words, they provide stability. Of course, there can be more legs, but at least three are needed! In other words, for your business or ministry to be successful, you only need to focus on three elements! Not five, not ten, just three!

Secondly, for the tabouret to be stable, the legs need to be of equal length! Having one, even a very "developed" leg, will not provide stability! You will constantly have to "catch" balance. In other words, even if one or two elements are well organized, but the third one is weaker, you need to pay attention to it and bring it up to the level of the others! Otherwise, you will occasionally face difficulties, connected with that weak element.

Thirdly, for the tabouret to be a tabouret, it needs a seat, which, on the one hand, serves to attach the legs and, on the other, defines the purpose of this object! Without the seat, it is just a set of sticks!

Each element of the tabouret corresponds to a certain area of activity — this is "The Tabouret Principle"! If you manage to fully implement it, you will not only feel confident and be able to attract the best specialists to your team, you will also be able to establish a balance between work and personal life, and really influence your environment! Moreover, a business or ministry built in this way is likely to become something that will have a sustainable, positive impact on the world around it!

Next, we will break down each element in detail — what each leg and the seat represents. Furthermore, during each breakdown, I will propose tasks that will help you not only better understand what each element of "The Tabouret Principle" means but also evaluate its level of implementation in your area of responsibility, and prepare plans for its integration into your business or ministry.

FOOD FOR THOUGHT

I've already mentioned that my study of the Bible coincided with my experience working in international corporations. Furthermore, I regularly participated in various training sessions, where I had the opportunity to become acquainted with the most advanced business and team management technologies. I regularly noticed that at the core of almost all corporate decisions lay Biblical truths. They are simply called "corporate policies" or "standards," and there is no reference to the original source! Moreover, while company founders (William Colgate, James Kraft, Johann Jacobs, ...) openly declared their faith and principles, nowadays there is a culture of "equal opportunities"! Having good relationships with company management, I tried to clarify the reason for this situation. While they agreed with me that the foundation of any successful corporate culture lies in Evangelical values, it's just not something that is openly discussed. One of the reasons for this is that corporations do business worldwide and have subsidiaries in countries where the dominant religion is Islam, Judaism, Buddhism, or any other religion. They cannot afford to openly speak about the Gospel because it might harm the business and provoke accusations of discrimination. At first, I was swept away by a wave of indignation: "How can you be so spineless? You have the resources and influence that could change the lives of millions of people!"

After some time, I was able to look at this issue from another perspective. During the Last Supper, one of the truths that Jesus shared with His disciples was the truth about love and how others would recognize them:

A new command I give you: Love one another. As I have loved you,
so you must love one another. By this everyone will know that you
are my disciples, if you love one another.
— John 13:34-35

· Alex Marchuk ·

Do you understand? We will not be recognized on the streets because we hang a big cross around our neck, wear clothing with Christian symbols, perform certain rituals, or preach to everyone about Jesus... Perhaps you've met people who prayed or preached loudly and emotionally, but then did something completely contrary to Evangelical values?! How many situations are there where people, who initially spoke about their faith, later broke agreements, deadlines, or simply lied?! The English have a saying: "Your actions speak so loudly, I can't hear your words!" Only true brotherly love and relationships based on mutual respect and recognition of each person's gifts and talents can create an atmosphere that will attract and engage others!

As a teenager, I was once a member of a street gang. One of the reasons that attracted me to it was the idea that we supported each other! If someone from our group was hurt, we would gather together and punish the offender! The idea that you are not alone, that there are those who will support and help you, was a powerful unifying motive! Over time, I became more interested in sports and studies and "left" the gang. However, I still remember the time when we were together and stood by each other. By the way, this is one of the reasons why street gangs are so popular among teenagers. On the other hand, the lack of such community is one of the reasons for the decline in believers in churches. Building horizontal relationships among church members is an area where the church can strengthen itself and, as a result, increase its influence!

Thus, in my opinion, we should not rush to "convert everyone and anyone" to our faith. Before making the decision to repent and believe, everyone follows their own path, which is full of various situations and trials. If we truly want to fulfill our calling here on Earth, "**The Tabouret Principle**" can serve us well in this!

Ministry and Business: What's the Difference?

Do not be misled: "Bad company corrupts good character!"
—1 Corinthians 15:33

The next question that requires clarification is the difference between ministry and business. I have often heard the opinion that ideas or experiences that are successfully implemented in business are completely unsuitable for nonprofit projects or ministries. And conversely, what works in ministry doesn't work for business. Let's try to look into this question together.

If you repented some time ago and continue to attend a local church, you've probably noticed that although new people often join the church, they eventually disappear. Without analyzing or assessing the general organization of local congregations and how ministries are carried out, I propose looking at this situation from another perspective and, based on that, try to draw some conclusions together.

Every person who has accepted Jesus as their Saviour strives to dedicate time to prayer, studying the Word of God, and serving. In many believers, a stereotype has developed, suggesting that ministry can only take a certain form, which includes: worship, preaching, evangelism, giving, communal prayer, all of which take place in a specific location, such as a church, and are, moreover, voluntary. It is clear that, in addition to this, each of us also has the need to dedicate time to ourselves, our loved ones, our work (since we need to earn a living), leisure, and more...

Let's try to assess the time balance for the average believer with such a "traditional understanding of ministry". So, in a day, we have 24 hours. Seven days a week give us 168 hours.

Let's assume you have healthy sleep habits and you rest for 8 hours a day. Seven days multiplied by 8 hours gives us 56 hours of sleep a week.

From 168 hours, we subtract 56 hours of sleep, leaving us with 112 hours that each of us is awake and doing something throughout the week.

Now, let's assess how much time the average person spends on "ministry" in its traditional understanding. Typically, we can talk about the following:

- Sunday service — 2-3 hours

- Leadership meeting — 2-3 hours

- Home group — 2-3 hours

- Bible reading and prayer — 1 hour daily, which gives 7 hours a week (some may say this is an overestimate, but let's assume this is the case)

- Maybe a few more hours a week for other ministry — 2-3 hours

Altogether, this amounts to about 15-19 hours! From the 112 hours, we subtract this time, and we find that over 95 hours are spent interacting with the outside world!

15-19 hours versus 95 hours? The average believer spends roughly 6 times more time engaging with the world than in traditional "ministry" or fellowship with other believers! Now, recall that "bad company corrupts good character." If there is no supportive environment at home or work for the believer, there is a high likelihood that, over time, they will "cool down," stop dedicating time to studying the Bible, and eventually stop going to church! This is one of the reasons why people who enthusiastically come to repentance later disappear from the church.

Sometimes, there are reverse situations where newly converted people are so sincere and passionately ready to take on any tasks related to traditional "ministry" that they forget about their loved ones, home, and work. At the same time, this ministry is usually not rewarded materially. I once heard a grandiose phrase that "ministry is something for which you are willing to pay money!" Yet, they forget that the Word of God says:

For the Scripture says: "Do not muzzle an ox while it is treading out the grain," and "The worker deserves his wages."
— 1 Timothy 5:18

Unfortunately, this sometimes leads to misunderstandings, stress, and conflicts with loved ones. Of course, these situations can be avoided or their risks reduced if we understand what "ministry" truly is. If you are familiar with Strong's Concordance numbers, it will not be difficult for you to delve more thoroughly into the meaning of the word "ministry."

The first mention of this word is in the book of Exodus:

And he said, Certainly I will be with thee; and this shall be a token unto thee, that I have sent thee: When thou hast brought forth the people out of Egypt, ye shall SERVE God upon this mountain.
— Exodus 3:12

According to Strong's Concordance, the number of this word is 5647. The original word in Hebrew is עָבַד (pronounced: aw-bad'): to work, to labor; to cultivate, to till (the ground); to serve, to be a servant, to obey; to force or cause to work.

In the book of Numbers, we encounter another word:

The families of the sons of Kohath shall pitch on the side of the tabernacle southward. And the chief of the house of the father of the families of the Kohathites shall be Elizaphan the son of Uzziel. And their charge shall be the ark, and the table, and the candlestick, and the altars, and the vessels of the sanctuary wherewith they minister, and the hanging, and all the SERVICE thereof.
— Numbers 3:29-31

The number of this word is 8334. The original word in Hebrew is שָׁרַת (pronounced: shaw-rath'): to serve, to minister, to be on duty.

The next word, translated as "service", appears in the first book of Chronicles:

And their brethren, heads of the house of their fathers, a thousand and seven hundred and threescore; very able men for the work of the SERVICE of the house of God.
— 1 Chronicles 9:13

The number of this word is 5656. The original word in Hebrew is עֲבוֹדָה (pronounced: ab-o-daw'): service, work; slavery; ministry, usage.

You can find other words which were translated as "service" in other books of the Old Testament, but their meaning is similar to the above ones.

In the New Testament, the word for "serve" or "service" is also used several times. The first occurrence is in the Gospel of Matthew:

> *No man can serve two masters: for either he will hate the one, and love the other; or else he will hold to the one, and despise the other. Ye cannot SERVE God and mammon.*
> *— Matthew 6:24*

The number of this word is 1398. The original word in Greek is δουλεύω (pronounced: doo-lyoo-o): to be a slave; to serve, to perform the duties of a slave

In the same book, we find another word translated as "serve":

> *Just as the Son of Man did not come to be SERVED, but to SERVE, and to give His life as a ransom for many!*
> *— Matthew 20:28*

The number of this word is 1247. The original word in Greek is διακονία (pronounced: dee-ak-on-ee'-ah): service, ministry, duty, obligation; helper, assistance, charity; serving, waiting on (at table), hospitality.

This is the main word used in the New Testament to describe service.

Also, in the Gospel of Luke, we see the following:

> *That we, being delivered from the hand of our enemies, might SERVE Him without fear, In holiness and righteousness before Him all the days of our life.*
> *— Luke 1:74-75*

The number of this word is 3000. The original word in Greek is λατρεύω (pronounced: lat-ryoo'-o): service, work; worship, cult; life's duty; servant.

As we can see, the word "service" or "ministry" has a broader meaning than it is often interpreted. The common thread in all these definitions is that it's not about just a couple of hours a day. One could say that service refers to a way of life!

Let everything that has breath praise the Lord! Hallelujah!
— Psalm 150:6

How do the birds praise the Lord? When we wake up in the morning and hear the birds singing, our hearts are subconsciously filled with joy! How do domestic animals praise the Lord? They fulfill their functions: cows give milk, sheep — wool, dogs — protect and bring us joy... When I am asked about my service, I sincerely answer that I serve the Lord 24 hours a day, seven days a week! When you wake up in the morning, take your first conscious breath and... you start serving! Thank the Lord for the new day — you use your mouth to praise Him! While doing exercises, brushing your teeth, preparing breakfast — you hum psalms or hymns quietly to yourself, filling your mind with thoughts of the mercy and goodness of our Heavenly Creator! Serving breakfast to your family, cleaning the house, changing the diapers for your newborn or helping with the school tasks for your teenagers — everything can be part of your service to God! Even when you sleep — you can serve the Lord too: prophetic dreams, visions, or simply "a black screen" — all this can be service! God's Word encourages us to do everything as service:

And whatever you do, do it heartily, as to the Lord and not to men!
— Colossians 3:23

If we look at the definition of the word "service" in explanatory dictionaries, we see the following:

Serve (from Medieval Latin serviō, servīre, going back to Latin, "to perform duties for (a master) in the capacity of a slave, act in subservience, be at the service of,) — to be a servant; to be of use; to prove adequate or satisfactory.

So, "to serve" means to be useful to others! You can turn any task into a service if you do it consciously and with dedication to the Lord! Later, we will return to this idea to explore it more thoroughly.

FOOD FOR THOUGHT

Once, at the gates of a church, I saw a poster with the following message: "Service: Sunday at 10:00." From the perspective of an average person, it's clear that the people who gather here serve God once a week on Sunday. However, in my opinion, it would be more accurate to write "Gathering on Sunday at 10:00." Because serving God is something that happens outside the church, 24/7!

Reflective task:

If you look at serving as a way of life, what opportunities do you have to serve in relation to your loved ones? To your colleagues? To the community you are a part of? To strangers? Write down a few ideas related to serving for each of the mentioned groups.

Now, let's look at the definition of business in modern dictionaries:

Business — a usually commercial or mercantile activity engaged in as a means of livelihood; a commercial or sometimes an industrial enterprise; dealings or transactions especially of an economic nature.

The "commercial or mercantile activity" is directly related to money. So, business is about money. But what exactly is money?

> *A feast is made for laughter, and wine makes life merry, but money answers everything.*
> *— Ecclesiastes 10:19*

Often, you can hear something like this: "If I had money, then I would do this and that..." Sometimes it seems that without money, it's truly impossible to start anything or get by. But is that really the case? Is money really the driving force that enables self-realization and more?

I often asked the question "What is money?" to seminar participants, candidates in job interviews, and just to acquaintances. The answers varied. Some say that money is freedom, energy, power, strength, opportunities and resources. On the other hand, some say money is evil or just paper, and that it has no real value.

No matter what anyone says, one thing is clear: wherever we go and whatever we start doing, money becomes an important factor in obtaining certain benefits.

At the same time, these definitions don't give us an understanding of what money really is and, on the contrary, endow it with qualities it doesn't actually have. Moreover, these definitions don't explain what needs to be done to earn or multiply money. If money is freedom, what do I need to do to get it and to have more of it?

If we look at the dictionary definition, we will see the following:

Money — something generally accepted as a medium of exchange, a measure of value, or a means of payment; officially coined or stamped metal currency; wealth reckoned in terms of money; a form or denomination of coin or paper money.

In ancient times, there was barter exchange. For example, if you needed bread but you had fabric, you would have to create a certain chain of exchanges. You might exchange fabric for a horseshoe, then the horseshoe for a chicken, then the chicken for jewelry, and finally, you could exchange the jewelry for bread — if the bread owner was interested in receiving it. Money simplified these exchanges and made it possible to convert what you have into money and then exchange that money for what you need.

So, what does this definition of money give us? Actually, quite a lot.

First, it becomes clear that money doesn't come from nowhere. It is the result of exchange. In other words, money is a consequence, not a cause! The origin of money is exchange, and if there is no exchange, there is no money. To put it simply, money is the cart, not the horse. When you focus first on where to get money, you are essentially putting the cart in front of the horse! People who constantly think about where to get money are, often unconsciously, wasting time. Stop thinking about where to get money! Start focusing on the opportunities for exchange, i.e., what people around you need.

Second, for exchange to occur, two conditions must be met. First, there must be at least two parties involved in the exchange. Second, one of the parties must have a need, and the other party must either have or be interested in satisfying that need. Even if you don't have the exact product or service that another person needs, you can still act as a mediator and help the person satisfy their need through your knowledge of others who have the required goods or services. As a result of satisfying the need, an exchange occurs, and money is created. And you, as a mediator, can earn a commission!

Third, here's the recipe for making more money: You need to either increase the number of exchanges or increase the value of each exchange. For example, you could earn a million by selling millions of matchboxes and earning a small profit on each one, or you could, as a mediator, sell one airplane, and your commission from that sale might be much larger than the total earned from the matchboxes.

With this understanding of money, you can channel your energy and time into a constructive direction. By repeatedly applying this principle, you can increase the amount of money you have!

Reflective task:

Write down 3-5 ideas related to what, in your opinion, is needed by your family members and/or people around you.
How could you help them meet their needs?
Choose a few ideas that meet the following criteria:

· *You are well-versed in this field (you have the appropriate education or work experience in this field) or you know and trust people who are knowledgeable in this area.*

· *You know people who might need this.*

· *You know how to obtain/create the goods or services that are needed.*

· *You have an idea of the balance between costs and potential income.*

For one or more of the selected ideas, try to apply The Tabouret Principle and describe all the elements in detail. I am sure you will see interesting opportunities for their implementation!

To summarize, it can be noted that both types of activities — **Service (Ministry)** and **Business** — are aimed at meeting the needs of others!

FOOD FOR THOUGHT:

After resigning from my position as CEO of an international company, I became a co-founder of a company that sold massage equipment. I often heard remarks along the lines of "the decisions and practices 'there' don't work 'here'." My partners in the company were people who sincerely believed in God and considered that preaching the Gospel through business was one of the most effective ways to spread the Good News. I fully share this view on preaching the Gospel, and it became one of the most important reasons for me to engage in this business!

The company's business model was based on offering potential clients the opportunity to try out a massager for free, and as a result, they would realize that it not only provided a healing effect but was also simple, convenient, and accessible! Typically, a massage session lasted 10-15 minutes, during which consultants, most of whom were believers, had the chance to not only present the massage equipment but also get to know the clients better, often learning about their life circumstances and sharing their personal testimonies, encouraging, advising, and supporting them. Quite often, visitors, even if they didn't buy anything, left impressed with the visit and thanked the team and God for the encounter! This, by the way, is one of the working models of what is called "mission in business" or "business as a mission": the goal is not just to make a profit but also to impact people's lives and help them overcome difficult life circumstances.

I joined the company when there were already some branded stores. First, I visited them to meet the team and see how the work was organized. I met many passionate and dedicated people. Some stores had good sales, but others had results that didn't even cover the store's rent. To my surprise, I encountered that most often, the consultants from underperforming stores sincerely believed that the reason for this was their lack of dedication or, even worse, some kind of sin?! . How to deal with this? Right, they thought, more attention should be given to fasting, prayer, and reading the Bible! Instead of actively inviting mall visitors to try a free massage session and improving sales skills, employees prayed and fasted for better sales, and some read or listened to the Bible at their workplace…

We did a tremendous amount of work to help each team member become a true professional in sales. We developed and introduced standards that described all stages of store operations: deciding to launch, team recruitment and training, administration and financial accounting, sales and promotions, ordering, delivery, and equipment servicing…

As a result, the company achieved incredible success. In a few years, the number of stores grew to nearly 300, and the company's turnover exceeded 1 million dollars per month!

At the same time, our focus on service had its benefits. As a company, we once faced a situation where our supplier decided to "bypass" us and made a direct offer to our stores, which, in order to optimize their tax load, were registered as separate legal entities. So, can you imagine that despite the price being approximately 30% lower, more than 90% of our stores refused to cooperate with the supplier and continued working with our company? Why? Because for them, it was not just about selling and earning but about working with those who shared their passion for preaching the Gospel!

This is just one of many examples of how business and service can go hand in hand and complement each other.

Let's examine the key parameters of such activities and try to see how business and service differ from each other.

THE TARGET AUDIENCE

The Target Audience — is the intended audience or readership of a publication, advertisement, or other message catered specifically to the previously intended audience. In marketing and advertising, the target audience is a particular group of consumer within the predetermined target market, identified as the targets or recipients for a particular advertisement or message. (Wikipedia)

When talking about the target audience — whether in business or ministry — it refers to a group of people who need your product or service. In business, they are willing to pay for it. In ministry, however, the cost is usually covered by someone else.

Yet in both cases, the expectation remains the same: the needs of the target audience should be met! In business, this leads to "customer loyalty" and, as a result, repeat purchases. What about ministry? Ministers also expect a kind of "loyalty" — but in the form of feedback about the help provided and support, including joining the ministry in one way or another!

Furthermore, both business and ministry are interested in having their target audience share their experiences with their network — family, colleagues, and friends. The more people get involved, the greater the recognition, the wider the reach, and the stronger the impact! For business, this means increased revenue. For ministry, it's an opportunity to attract additional donors.

OPERATIONS MANAGEMENT

Operations Management — is concerned with designing and controlling the production of goods and services, ensuring that businesses are efficient in using resources to meet customer requirements. (Wikipedia)

Both in business and ministry, it's essential to carefully plan and organize how your products or services will reach the target audience.

- What products or services are needed to meet the needs of the target audience?
- How will these products or services be obtained or created? At what cost?
- How should their delivery and storage be organized?
- How will they become accessible to the target audience?

Answering these and other questions is crucial for managing both business and ministry effectively. Moreover, when addressing these questions, both business and ministry strive for maximum operational efficiency — that is, achieving the highest possible results with an optimal (reasonable) use of resources!

Efficiency — is the often measurable ability to avoid making mistakes or wasting materials, energy, efforts, money, and time while performing a task. In a more general sense, it is the ability to do things well, successfully, and without waste.

FOOD FOR THOUGHT

During Russia's invasion of Ukraine in 2022, I worked as a volunteer and led a charitable foundation. Throughout this time, I met many sincere and passionate people who were literally giving their last to support either refugees or our soldiers on the frontlines. I also had the privilege of working with several international charities and donors who, surprisingly, were sometimes more motivated to support Ukraine than some of our own citizens!

In the first two years of the war alone, our organization distributed over 7,000 tons of food, dozens of industrial generators, water purification systems, a boat, and thousands of units of clothing, footwear, and medical supplies. I'm thankful to the Lord for the opportunity to be part of such projects.

At the same time, I encountered several situations of glaring inefficiency.

For example, after the destruction of the Kakhovka Dam, many areas of the Kherson region faced a serious shortage of drinking water. One donor from Germany responded by sending several truckloads of bottled water from Germany to Kherson. I praise the Lord for the generosity and desire to help people in Ukraine. However, just imagine — the cost of delivery exceeded the value of the water itself! Could this issue have been solved differently? Of course! Either by purchasing the water locally or by acquiring water purification systems (like the ones our organization purchased).

In the first scenario, considering the price difference between water in Germany (which is higher) and Ukraine, plus the logistics costs, we could have bought nearly 3–4 times more drinking water! In the second scenario, a water purification system with a capacity of 500 liters per hour — costing roughly the same as a truckload of water — would have produced an equivalent amount of water in less than a week! Plus, the system would have continued to provide water long after.

Another case involved helping refugees with winter clothing. A donor sent a truckload of second-hand clothes from Europe to Ukraine. Again, praise the Lord that the needs of Ukrainians touched hearts in Europe! However, it turned out that some of the clothes were so worn out they could only be used as rags. Some were not winter clothes at all. Only about 40–50% of the shipment was actually distributed to those in need. And again — consider the cost of delivery...

Business is interested in maximum efficiency because it directly impacts profit. In the case of ministry, maximum efficiency allows you to reach a larger target audience with the same budget!

RESOURCES

Resource — a source of supply or support; a natural source of wealth or revenue —often used in plural; a natural feature or phenomenon that enhances the quality of human life; a source of information or expertise.

We've already mentioned the importance of money. However, besides money, you also need staff, technology, contacts and connections, and material and technical resources. To implement any project, you need to find a way to either pay for or otherwise secure the necessary resources.

In business, the owners either invest their own funds, secures bank loans, or raises money by selling shares in the business.

In ministry, funding usually comes from either the personal funds of ministers or from donors — organizations interested in addressing specific social issues. If your project's goals align with the mission of a particular international charity, you can apply for funding from that organization and potentially secure the necessary support.

When it comes to resources like staff, both business and ministry require qualified and motivated team members. It's a mistake to think that just because business offers a salary, non-material motivation isn't needed! We've all seen cases where employees, even with relatively high pay, performed their work carelessly.

On the other hand, just because it's a ministry doesn't mean the material aspect is irrelevant for participants! As the Bible says:

> For it is written in the Law of Moses: "You shall not muzzle an ox
> while it treads out the grain." Is it for oxen that God is concerned?
> — 1 Corinthians 9:9

Each of us is a living person, and we need money to cover our food, clothing, household needs, and leisure...

It's disheartening to see how many believers spend their time and resources on ministry, only to later worry about how to meet their basic needs. Leading charitable organizations have long recognized this, and for all their employees involved in various projects, they ensure decent compensation. This approach, by the way, allows them to attract top-tier specialists, which leads to high effectiveness and outstanding results from such organizations!

As we can see, the task of attracting the necessary resources overlaps in both cases — business and ministry!

FOOD FOR THOUGHT

Lately, there's been a lot of speculation about robots and artificial intelligence completely replacing human labor. Is this true? Will most of the professions we are familiar with vanish in the near future, and will people lose their ability to earn a living? There are many professions and types of work that truly don't require special skills or qualifications from workers. However, there are also fields where people themselves diminish their uniqueness and do everything necessary to be replaced by machines.

One business I once founded was a chain of coffee shops. Given that we roasted our own high-quality coffee beans, had excellent professional equipment, and prime locations with high foot traffic, one would expect that each coffee shop would show high sales and profits. However, sales and profits were not only determined by these factors but also by the performance of individual staff members (baristas). When I was involved in the day-to-day management of the company, I often noticed that there were baristas who would notice customers right at the door, establish eye contact, smile, and politely take orders. They would prepare drinks quickly and cheerfully, exchanging pleasantries along the way, and serve the drinks with a smile and best wishes.

On the other hand, there were those who were physically present at work but seemed mentally far away. They didn't notice customers, engaged with them without enthusiasm, took a long time to prepare orders, and handed them out without any emotion. As a rule, these baristas always had lower sales and profits.

My observations and work with the team led me to an interesting conclusion. Perhaps you've often heard this verse from God's Word:

But do you want to know, O foolish man, that faith without works is dead?
— James 2:20

Faith without works is dead, that's true. However, works without faith are is just routine! If you do something and it doesn't inspire you, if it doesn't give you a sense of self-fulfillment and meaningful life, then, as a rule, you're just mechanically going through the motions, and that really gives reason for a robot to replace you! Understand that the competitive advantage of a person over a robot lies in our ability to do something with passion, to give emotions, to create an atmosphere, to show empathy! Understand that it's not just 'about money.' It's your life! You only have one! There won't be another! Do what you love! Change the world for the better! Do good! As a result, you will not only earn an income but, most importantly, find peace in your heart and satisfaction with yourself!

RESULT

Result — something that results as a consequence, issue, or conclusion; something obtained by calculation or investigation

From the definition of business, it follows that the result is profit, which arises because the costs of implementing business processes are lower than the revenue received from the client. This is possible when the client's needs are met through the product or service, and they choose a particular business over many other competing options.

In the case of ministry, the result is the achievement of goals for which donor funds were raised.

In both cases, the key components of the result also include a sense of dignity, satisfaction, respect, and recognition from others, as well as receiving material goods. With the exception of profit, the remaining components overlap for both business and ministry!

ADMINISTRATION

Administration — performance of executive duties; the act or process of administering something.

Both business and ministry operate in environments regulated by laws, which include specific taxes and reporting requirements. The fact that ministry does not generate income does not exempt its leader from providing reports to the relevant government institutions. Of course, in the case of ministry, the volume of reporting is smaller, the frequency is less, and the format is simpler. However, both types of organizations are required to report on their activities to the relevant authorities.

Moreover, one of the key issues in ministry is the relationship with donors. Every donor wants to be assured that the funds allocated for the ministry have been used correctly and effectively! Donors, in turn, must report to those who directly donated the funds. Therefore, each ministry prepares photo and video reports, creates lists of people who received assistance, and backs up expenses with corresponding receipts or invoices.

Let's summarize the above thoughts:

	Business	**Ministry**
Target Audience	Matters	Matters
Resources	Own Attracted (loan or sale of a share)	Own Attracted (donors)
Operational Activity	Focus on maximum efficiency	Focus on maximum efficiency
Result	Achieving goals (profit) Recognition Respect and dignity	Achieving goals (as agreed) Recognition Respect and dignity
Administration	Accounting Report for shareholders	Accounting Report for donors

As can be seen from the above considerations, business and ministry have much more in common than they differ. Therefore, from now on, I will use the term "project" and assume that the ideas presented are applicable to both business and ministry!

Some may still continue to "demonize" business and money. In such a case, I suggest asking yourself a question: Is a guitar evil or good? If the guitar is in the hands of a band member who praises the devil, it is, in essence, connected to evil. But if the guitar is in the hands of a worship team in a church, then it is connected to good. What is the point of this example? It's to show that business and money, just like a guitar, are merely tools. How these tools are used depends on whose hands they are in! If a person is unaware and unconscious, then alcohol, drugs, weapons, prostitution, pornography... are simply ways of making a profit. But if a person is aware and devoted, they will use available tools to make the world around them and the lives of others better!

Earlier, we discussed the distribution of time between ministry and other tasks throughout the week. How can we change the time distribution to benefit the ministry? One solution is to fill those 95 hours with Gospel content! To bring a different understanding of the word "ministry"! To make it so that even while doing household or work tasks, you are still, in one way or another, interacting with the Lord and fulfilling His will! Is this possible? Of course, it is! For some, this may sound new, but this approach is to "do business (work) as ministry." This became one of the key principles of the Protestant movement, formulated by Martin Luther. Literally, Martin Luther said: "A Christian who makes shoes fulfills his Christian duty not when he cuts a cross on the shoe, but when he makes good shoes, because God is interested in a good craftsman."

Other names are used for this approach: Mission in Business, Business as Mission. It doesn't matter what it is called, the essence of this approach boils down **"to weaving the thread of Gospel meanings into the fabric of everyday life and business processes"** ! It's not about studying the Bible or praying all day. Nor is it about telling everyone that we are Christians. We're not even talking about using Christian symbols, like crosses, in the design everywhere. Not at all! So, how will those who interact with us — our employees, our suppliers and contractors, our clients — understand that our business has a mission?

The answers to this question will be addressed in each chapter of this book. I sincerely hope that by the time you finish reading **"The Tabouret Principle",** you will understand how you can implement this in your field of activity.

SUMMARY OF THE CHAPTER "MINISTRY AND BUSINESS: WHAT'S THE DIFFERENCE?"

Ministry is not about a few hours a week. It's a way of living!

At the core of the definition of Ministry and Business lies the desire to meet the needs of others.

Mission in business or Business as mission is an effective way to combine business and service, allowing not only to make a profit but also to spread the Gospel.

Reflective task:

Based on the information received, note down what you could share with your loved ones or colleagues. Plan a meeting, share, and discuss your thoughts.

_____

_____

_____

_____

_____

_____

_____

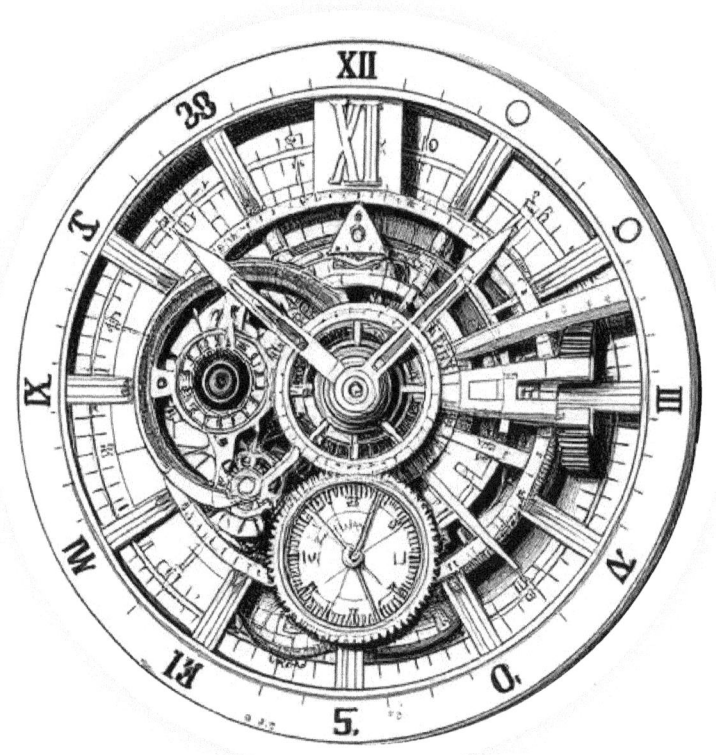

The First Leg of the Tabouret Principle: the System

In the beginning God created the heaven and the earth. And the earth was without form, and void; and darkness was upon the face of the deep. And the Spirit of God moved upon the face of the waters. And God said, Let there be light: and there was light. And God saw the light, that it was good: and God divided the light from the darkness. And God called the light Day, and the darkness he called Night. And the evening and the morning were the first day. And God said, Let there be a firmament in the midst of the waters, and let it divide the waters from the waters. And God made the firmament, and divided the waters which were under the firmament from the waters which were above the firmament: and it was so. And God called the firmament Heaven. And the evening and the morning were the second day. And God said, Let the waters under the heaven be gathered together unto one place, and let the dry land appear: and it was so. And God called the dry land Earth; and the gathering together of the waters called he Seas: and God saw that it was good. And God said, Let the earth bring forth grass, the herb yielding seed, and the fruit tree yielding fruit after his kind, whose seed is in itself, upon the earth: and it was so. And the earth brought forth grass, and herb yielding seed after his kind, and the

• Alex Marchuk •

tree yielding fruit, whose seed was in itself, after his kind: and God saw that it was good. And the evening and the morning were the third day. And God said, Let there be lights in the firmament of the heaven to divide the day from the night; and let them be for signs, and for seasons, and for days, and years: And let them be for lights in the firmament of the heaven to give light upon the earth: and it was so. And God made two great lights; the greater light to rule the day, and the lesser light to rule the night: he made the stars also. And God set them in the firmament of the heaven to give light upon the earth, And to rule over the day and over the night, and to divide the light from the darkness: and God saw that it was good. And the evening and the morning were the fourth day. And God said, Let the waters bring forth abundantly the moving creature that hath life, and fowl that may fly above the earth in the open firmament of heaven. And God created great whales, and every living creature that moveth, which the waters brought forth abundantly, after their kind, and every winged fowl after his kind: and God saw that it was good. And God blessed them, saying, Be fruitful, and multiply, and fill the waters in the seas, and let fowl multiply in the earth. And the evening and the morning were the fifth day. And God said, Let the earth bring forth the living creature after his kind, cattle, and creeping thing, and beast of the earth after his kind: and it was so. And God made the beast of the earth after his kind, and cattle after their kind, and every thing that creepeth upon the earth after his kind: and God saw that it was good.
— *Genesis 1:1-25*

The Bible begins with an extraordinary and captivating story of the creation of the Earth and everything that fills it and surrounds it. Considering how each element interacts with one another and how this interaction repeats over time, this is our first leg of the Tabouret Principle — the System.

The System (comes from the Latin word systēma, in turn from Greek σύστημα systēma: "whole concept made of several parts or members, system", literary "composition") — is a group of interacting or interrelated elements that act according to a set of rules to form a unified whole. A system, surrounded and influenced by its environment, is described by its boundaries, structure and purpose and is expressed in its functioning.

Or, in other words, we can say that a system is a set of processes that repeat over time and produce a certain predictable result.

God's system works flawlessly. We may not even realize it, but every moment, billions of processes are taking place in our bodies, involving the formation of new cells and the breakdown of old ones! Day follows night, and the seasons cycle one after another. If you sow wheat, you will reap wheat! A peach pit can only grow into a peach tree, and a cow can only give birth to a calf! Planets and constellations move in their orbits, allowing us to predict their positions with precision over time!

Virtually everything in our bodies and the surrounding world operates through systematic processes, the result of which is the existence of the project called "life on Earth". We don't have to consciously think about producing a certain number of red blood cells or secreting specific substances for stomach acid formation — it all happens autonomously. Similarly, most natural phenomena, from the microscopic world to the behavior of galaxies, follow this pattern…

Now, imagine that the same clear and perfect system operates within your projects! Sounds reasonable, right? No matter what project you're working on, as a leader, it's essential to achieve a clear and predictable result through a series of repeatable actions.

FOOD FOR THOUGHT

"System beats class!" — A comment made during a football match between Germany and Brazil, when the Germans, thanks to their more organized play, managed to defeat the more technically skilled Brazilians.

Let's consider System through the approach to project management.

Project (from Latin projectus — "thrown forward") — a unique set of processes, limited by time, resources, and quality requirements, aimed at creating new value.

Among the various approaches to defining types of projects, there is one that divides all projects into two main types: Original and Standard.

Original projects are those that, either entirely or partially, are being carried out for the first time. In the above section from the Book of Genesis, this can be associated with the phrase: "And God said: … and it happened…", meaning something that didn't exist before came into being because the Lord "said"! Imagine you are an architect, and you need to build a house. An original project means you have to design everything from scratch! The foundation, utilities, walls, interiors... Agree, even for an experienced professional, this task is no easy feat!

Standard projects are repetitive projects that are carried out again, with all stages clearly described and documented. Drawing a parallel with the Biblical quote above: "And the earth brought forth grass, the herb that yields seed according to its kind, and the tree that yields fruit, whose seed is in itself according to its kind." In other words, both grass and trees have seeds that allow them to bear fruit according to their kind! Thus, neither grass nor trees need to "invent" how to multiply — the seed contains the blueprint for what it will grow into! Returning to the example of building a house, in the case of a standard project, you receive a ready-made design that has been implemented many times in other places, where everything has been taken into account and thoroughly tested.

In project management, to evaluate the success of a project's execution, the abbreviation **"C.G.B."** is often used and its meaning is as follows:

C — Condition or **Quality**: Within any project, it is expected that the result will meet certain requirements.

G — Graphic (Schedule) or **Timeline**: Every project has a beginning, an end, and implementation stages that are defined over time.

B — Budget or **Cost Estimate**: Projects usually require specific expenditures that need to be controlled.

According to research conducted by The Standish Group Inc. (USA), the success statistics of project implementation from the perspective of **C.G.B.** are as follows:

	Original projects	Standard projects
Projects were implemented with 100% fulfilment of the CGB	16%	76%
Projects were implemented with a violation of one of CGB criteria	53%	20%
Projects weren't implemented at all	31%	4%

Considering these results, the following conclusions become obvious:

Which type of projects are much more advantageous to deal with?

Of course, Standard projects! The number of successfully implemented Standard projects is almost 5 times higher than the corresponding figure for Original projects! The number of unfinished projects is almost 8 times lower than for Original projects!

So why are Original projects needed at all?

Without them, there would be no progress! By falling and getting up, we learned to walk. Through trial and error, we can make things better, reducing costs and/or increasing returns! This is the role Original projects can play. You do something different, something new. You get a result. You compare it with historical data. If the result exceeds the historical data in certain parameters and you are satisfied, then perhaps you have found a way to improve your project and increase its returns.

How can we increase the benefits of Original projects?

One way or another, some of us, even within the framework of a Standard project, have to perform certain tasks for the first time. And it's normal if, during these tasks, one or more **C.G.B.** criteria are violated. What is important when dealing with an Original project? It's important to describe it and turn it into a Standard project! The most crucial thing when carrying out Original projects is to describe the sequence of actions and thus turn them into Standard projects in the future! In this case, even if the project is not successfully completed, it won't just be a waste of time and money, but an investment in making sure you can implement it at a completely different level in the future!

What advantages do Standard projects provide?

Just imagine, you don't have to spend time and resources to find the best solution to a particular problem! Someone else has taken care of this for you, "learned from mistakes", tried different options, and gave you the most optimal one! Moreover, if there are any changes in the team and a new employee joins, you won't need to spend much time bringing them up to speed! Of course, you will have to communicate with the new team member, but at least you won't need to explain basic things that are already described in work standards, job descriptions, etc.

Thus, anyone who wants to successfully implement their project and turn it into something scalable that can influence the world around them faces the task of **turning Original projects into Standard ones!**

What distinguishes Standard projects from Original ones?

Let's explore this using the example of a computer.

1. ALGORITHMS

Every computer runs on an **operating system** — a set of algorithms that precisely and **definitively** define each operation.

Definitive — serving to define or specify precisely.

For example, each key corresponds to a specific algorithm that produces a **definitive** result. Imagine how difficult it would be to work on a computer that gives a different outcome every time you press the same key! Therefore, one of the key properties that an **Algorithm** provides is **definitiveness** — every specific action must produce a predictable result! It's unacceptable for a single action to lead to multiple different outcomes! We can find biblical examples that confirm this principle. Consider the consequences when Adam broke God's command or what happened to Aaron's sons when they brought unauthorized fire into the Holy of Holies. In each case, strict adherence to the instruction was required — and who knows how history might have unfolded if those instructions had been followed?!

2. CRITERIA OR INDICATORS

Any algorithm must have a **criterion** that defines its progress.

In the example of a computer, you can notice that it has a keyboard with labeled letters or numbers. By pressing them, we expect a certain outcome. When you press a particular key, you consciously expect a specific command to be executed. The key labels are an example of **Criteria**. Of course, it's important that the person pressing the keys understands the language used for the labels. For instance, if the keys are labeled with Japanese characters and the person is unfamiliar with them, the **Criteria** will be meaningless! However, if the language is known, then regardless of who is using the computer — a man, a woman, an elderly person, or a child — the criteria will be perceived in the same way! In other words, when defining **Criteria**, it's crucial that they are **consistent** and **objective**.

Consistent — marked by harmony, regularity, or steady continuity; free from variation or contradiction.

Objective — expressing or dealing with facts or conditions as perceived without distortion by personal feelings, prejudices, or interpretations.

3. MONITORING

It's not enough to simply know which **criteria** define a process and provide insight into its dynamics — you also need to understand **how** and **how regularly** these criteria can be tracked! In the computer example, every device has a screen or monitor that immediately displays the results of our interaction with the computer. Thanks to this, we can see how well the interaction is progressing. If there's an error, we can correct it right away. The computer screen serves as an example of **Monitoring**. Moreover, the screen is positioned right in front of our eyes, so we don't have to make any effort or waste time to see it. In other words, **Monitoring** should be organized in such a way that the information is both timely and accessible!

Timely — coming early or at the right time; appropriate or adapted to the times or the occasion.

Accessible — capable of being reached; easy to speak to or deal with; capable of being used or seen.

Thus, there are three key differences between **Original** and **Standard** projects:

1. **Algorithms**

2. **Criteria**

3. **Monitoring**

Next, we will explore each of these elements in greater detail.

The First Leg of the Tabouret Principle: the System — Algorithms

Algorithm (from Arabic al-khuwārizmi, from al-Khwārizmī flourished a.d. 825 Islamic mathematician) — a procedure for solving a mathematical problem (as of finding the greatest common divisor) in a finite number of steps that frequently involves repetition of an operation; a step-by-step procedure for solving a problem or accomplishing some end

If you can confidently answer "yes" to the statements below, it means that this component of successful work is, to some extent, implemented in your project:

- There are detailed work standards for each employee and every area of activity.

- Job descriptions are clearly defined.

- A clear organizational structure exists within the company.

- There are no "blind spots" in the interaction between departments.

And let them make me a sanctuary; that I may dwell among them. According to all that I shew thee, after the pattern of the tabernacle, and the pattern of all the instruments thereof, even so shall ye make it.
— Exodus 25:8-9

The Bible is filled with detailed descriptions of various devices, rituals, and projects: God's command to Adam regarding the fruits of the garden, Noah's instructions for building the ark, Joseph's plan for storing grain in Egypt, the instructions for the Passover lamb, the laws and regulations, the organization of temple service, and the order of the Lord's Supper — these are just a few examples of **Algorithms** described in the Bible. Therefore, it is completely natural for us to draw wisdom and knowledge from the Bible on how different processes should be organized!

In this specific example, **Moses** was not simply imagining things and constructing the tabernacle as he pleased. Not at all! He received clear instructions — **Algorithms** — directly from the Lord. Moreover, the Lord commanded Moses to follow those instructions **precisely**.

Whether you already have an active project or are just planning to start one, you need to make sure that your project is built on **Algorithms**! The absence of a system means that you or your employees will handle recurring tasks in different ways each day. As a result, some tasks will be completed less efficiently, resources (from raw materials to time) will be wasted, the quality of goods or services may decline, and ultimately, you risk losing customers.

Moreover, the lack of **Algorithms** significantly undermines the potential for continuity and growth. Hiring and onboarding new employees becomes a lengthy and often chaotic process — similar to trying to teach someone to swim by simply pushing them into deep water! If they manage to stay afloat — great! If not — well, they're just not the right fit!

And what about resignations, illnesses, or even something as simple as employee vacations? In some cases, these situations create serious challenges for both projects and their managers! It's also important to note that such situations are often linked to high levels of stress, which, in turn, lead to conflicts and arguments, a tense and anxious atmosphere within the team, reduced productivity and motivation, and ultimately, emotional and physical burnout.

On the other hand, having **Algorithms** allows you to expect consistent results and the overall development of the project!

If we reflect on how the Lord created the Earth, we can see that everything was done in **sequence**. He didn't create humans or animals first and then try to figure out where to place them. First, He created the heavens and the earth, light, the universe, the sun, and the moon. Fish were created after rivers, seas, and oceans were established — not the other way around. Animals were created after plants had already been made, so they would have food to eat.

In the same way, we need to define the **sequence of stages**, detail each one, and identify which actions will enable us to influence the entire project moving forward. We need to move from the **general to the specific**, paying close attention to ensuring that each step is clearly defined.

Therefore, all actions within any project can be broadly divided into **three key stages**:

1. **Identifying** your target audience and understanding their needs — the specific problems that your product or service can solve.

2. **Creating** (or acquiring) a product or service designed to meet those identified needs.

3. **Delivering** the product or service to the target audience to satisfy those needs and, if necessary, **handling payment** or any other form of exchange.

From my experience, depending on the specific situation, the **first and second stages** can be swapped. You can either:

- Research your target audience to identify their needs and then find ways to satisfy them, **or**

- Start with existing products or services and consciously search for a target audience that might need them.

These three stages form a kind of **cycle**, after which you return to the first stage and repeat the process. Just as God created the cyclic nature of day and night, the seasons, and the water cycle, we also develop a **cyclic interaction** with our target audience.

FOOD FOR THOUGHT

At one of the business management and strategic planning trainings conducted by my colleagues from the United States, an interesting concept was introduced under the phrase: "First, consider the MOST."

This phrase can be understood as: "First, consider the main thing." On its own, the phrase makes sense. But, being Americans, they naturally embedded additional meaning to clarify what exactly is hidden behind this "main thing."

The word "MOST" is an acronym representing the following key business areas:

Marketing — The organizational function and the set of processes for creating, promoting, and delivering a product or service to customers and managing customer relationships in a way that benefits the organization.

Operations — The organization's activities related to producing and delivering goods or services according to the purpose and goals of the business.

Sales — The business concept describing the final stage of the business cycle, involving the exchange of a product or service for money, confirmed by a sales receipt, a completion certificate, or a delivery note.

Technology — The set of methods and tools that, based on existing knowledge, create opportunities to solve practical problems and achieve desired results, while providing a competitive advantage compared to similar projects.

Therefore, to ensure your project thrives, you need to focus on organizing and systematizing these four areas of activity. As a leader, you must honestly assess the current state of affairs — only with a clear and realistic understanding can you make meaningful improvements!

As I often remind myself: **It doesn't matter where you are right now. What matters is knowing where you're going and what you need to do to get there!**

First, within each stage, you need to identify the **key actions**. To demonstrate this approach more clearly, let's look at an example of the process for creating a product in a company that specializes in coffee roasting. To start, you need to highlight the key actions — that is, the **sequence of steps** required to produce the product or service. This should be based on your experience and common sense. Let me point out right away that this description is by no means fixed or final. Over time, as your product or service evolves, market conditions shift, and work processes improve or other circumstances change, you may adjust or refine your key actions accordingly. The most important thing is to have a clear understanding of the **sequence of steps** that will lead you to the desired outcome!

№	Key actions				
1	Creating (or acquiring) a product or service:				
1-1	1. Defining the green coffee supplier				
1-2	2. Purchasing and delivering green coffee				
1-3	3. Roasting and packaging the coffee				
1-4	4. Moving the coffee to the finished goods warehouse				

Reflective task:

For your project, identify one product or service (I recommend choosing the one that generates the highest revenue) and outline the key actions involved in its creation (or acquisition).

After outlining the actions required to create a product or service, we need to break down each action in detail and list the specific steps for each one.

№	Key actions	Steps			
1	Creating (or acquiring) a product or service:				
1-1	1. Defining the green coffee supplier	1. Establishing contact with suppliers 2. Receiving information about stock availability 3. Negotiating price and delivery terms			
1-2	2. Purchasing and delivering green coffee	1. Receiving the invoice 2. Payment 3. Delivery			
1-3	3. Roasting and packaging the coffee	1. Roasting a sample 2. Roasting a batch 3. Degassing and packaging			
1-4	4. Moving the coffee to the finished goods warehouse	1. Preparing the invoice 2. Moving the product to the warehouse			

Reflective task:

For the product or service you have chosen, write down the specific steps involved in its creation (or acquisition).

_____

_____

_____

_____

_____

_____

_____

_____

_____

By following a similar approach for all other processes, we can develop a set of algorithms that will describe the actions and steps at each stage to achieve the desired result.

Let me remind you once again that our task is to use algorithms to transform every process within the organization into a "Standard Project." Most tasks are repeated day after day, and we need to ensure that, based on our experience, we define the most effective way to complete each task. This will minimize the risk of something being done incorrectly.

By describing algorithms, we are essentially defining the **Standards** for performing specific actions in a way that delivers the desired result with minimal costs.

Standard — something established by authority, custom, or general consent as a model or example; something set up and established by authority as a rule for the measure of quantity, weight, extent, value, or quality.

In many companies, standards define not only work processes but also how employees or the office (or retail outlet) should look, how communication should be conducted, and how certain decisions should be made.

A set of such standard actions is usually combined into **Job Descriptions**, which serve as a guide for employees. It is perfectly logical for warehouse management tasks to be handled by a warehouse manager, accounting and tax records to be managed by an accountant, sales to be handled by a sales manager, and production-related tasks to be addressed by a production specialist, and so on.

Job Descriptions — an orderly record of the essential activities involved in the performance of a task that is abstracted from a job analysis and used in classifying and evaluating jobs and in the selection and placement of employees

With detailed algorithms and standards in hand, you can more objectively assess the required qualifications of an employee, the workload, and, accordingly, the time spent. You can also see how various positions are interconnected, and as a result, you can proceed to the creation or revision of what is known as the **Organizational chart** of the company.

Organizational chart — a graphic display of reporting relationships in an organization, sometimes displaying position titles and position holders.

With a clear **Organizational chart** of the project in hand, you will be able to describe the order of interaction between departments and avoid situations where one department completes its task, but the next one does not pick it up. This way, you eliminate the "white spots" between departments and ensure smooth operation, where every detail receives attention.

№	Key actions	Steps	Responsible		
1	Creating (or acquiring) a product or service:				
1-1	1. Defining the green coffee supplier	1. Establishing contact with suppliers 2. Receiving information about stock availability 3. Negotiating price and delivery terms	The technologist is responsible for preparing the information, while the director approves it.		
1-2	2. Purchasing and delivering green coffee	1. Receiving the invoice 2. Payment 3. Delivery	The accountant is responsible for receiving and paying the invoice, while the logistics manager is responsible for the delivery of raw materials.		
1-3	3. Roasting and packaging the coffee	1. Roasting a sample 2. Roasting a batch 3. Degassing and packaging	The technologist is responsible for the entire cycle.		

№	Key actions	Steps	Responsible		
1-4	4. Moving the coffee to the finished goods ware-house	1. Preparing the invoice 2. Moving the product to the warehouse	The technologist pre-pares the product and the delivery note. The accountant registers the delivery note in the accounting system. The logistics specialist handles the physical movement.		

FOOD FOR THOUGHT:

Today, there are special Business Process Management Software (BPMS) programs that help make the process of describing algorithms more visual and organized. The choice of a specific program depends on your business activity, size, and region. Moreover, some programs also offer AI-based assistant support. These programs are usually available on a subscription basis with a monthly fee. The most popular programs include:

- Monday.com
- Integrify
- Pneumatic Workflow
- Pipedrive
- Kintone

Typically, such applications categorize business processes into three types: **core, management,** and **supporting** processes.

1. **Core processes** are related to activities that generate profit or are the reason for the company's existence. In other words, these are all algorithms aimed at creating and promoting goods or services.

2. **Supporting processes** are essential for the realization of Core processes and are related to the provision of resources and record-keeping, such as logistics, human resources, accounting, and IT.

3. **Management processes** are conditionally positioned above Core and Supporting processes as they are linked to strategic management of the company, setting directions for development, and determining goals.

Usually, business process descriptions begin with identifying all the operations within the company and breaking them down into types (core, supporting, management).

Each process has the following components:

- **Input** — the resource that triggers the start of the process (information, raw materials, etc.)
- **Output** — the result of the process
- **Owner** — the person responsible for achieving the planned outcome, making adjustments, and improving the process
- **Supplier** — the person who provides the input resource for the process
- **Consumer or Client** — those interested in the result of the process, who can be internal consumers (company employees) or external (clients, suppliers, partners).

Processes are typically described on several levels. In the simplest version, there are two levels: upper and lower. The upper level provides an overall description without going into detail, while the lower level breaks down each process into subprocesses and individual procedures.

Processes are first described in their current state, and then, taking into account gaps and discrepancies, a vision of how they should be is created.

For process description, there are specific notations (EPC, BPMN, IDEF0, etc.) — graphical representations of business processes that serve as the basis for detailed descriptions of each process, visual depictions, the creation of process cards, and flowcharts for each process, and so on.

As a result, you will get a visual representation of each process, where it is clear who is responsible, who interacts with whom, which resources are needed, what is required to achieve the desired outcome, and most importantly — how this process can be improved.

Reflective task:

For the product or service you have chosen, specify the person responsible for each step according to the action algorithm.

The First Leg of the Tabouret Principle: the System — Criteria

Criteria (from Greek kritérion "to separate, choose, decide, judge") — a standard on which a judgment or decision may be based; a characterizing mark or trait.

If you can confidently answer "yes" to the statements below, it means that this component of successful work is, to some extent, implemented in your project:

· Every team member knows which Criteria are used to evaluate their work results.

· All Criteria are objective.

· The Criteria used to evaluate managers are based on key criteria of the subordinate employees.

· The project or department manager uses consolidated Criteria and can decompose them if necessary to identify deviations.

And they shall take of the blood, and strike it on the two side posts
and on the upper door post of the houses, wherein they shall eat
it… And the blood shall be to you for a token upon the houses
where ye are: and when I see the blood, I will pass over you, and
the plague shall not be upon you to destroy you, when I smite the
land of Egypt.
— Exudes 12:7, 13

In the description of the plagues for the Egyptians, the last, tenth plague — the death of the firstborns — occurred. In every house where there was no blood on the doorposts, someone died. The presence of blood on the doorposts was a Criterion that marked the "chosen" and served as a signal for the Angel of Death. Another well-known Criterion was the sheep's skin — Gideon repeatedly asked the Lord to confirm His selection.

Each day of creation ended with God the Creator evaluating what had been done and emphasizing that it was good. Based on what could He say this? Based on the fact that the result of His work was real transformations, which had an objective nature and which we can currently see around us.

FOOD FOR THOUGHT:

Two pilots are flying a plane. One of them says to the other: "Criteria?"

The other replies: "Twenty-five!"

The first one asks: "What does 'twenty-five' mean?"

And the second replies: "What does 'Criteria' mean?"

Usually I say: "What cannot be measured, cannot be improved!"

It's hard to deny the existence of day and night, the seasons, the planets, and the constellations… Regardless of who evaluates it — an adult or a child, a man or a woman, an educated person or not — they will have to admit that it exists! That's why it's written in the Epistle to the Romans:

For the wrath of God is revealed from heaven against all ungodliness
and unrighteousness of men, who hold the truth in unrighteousness;
Because that which may be known of God is manifest in them; for
God hath shewed it unto them. For the invisible things of him from

the creation of the world are clearly seen, being understood by the things that are made, even his eternal power and Godhead; so that they are without excuse: Because that, when they knew God, they glorified him not as God, neither were thankful; but became vain in their imaginations, and their foolish heart was darkened.
— Romans 1:18-21

Criteria play an important role not only in projects but also in each of our lives. Should you take a fever reducer or not? Your body temperature will tell you. Generally, if it's below 38°C, it's better not to lower it — the body's immune system can handle the inflammatory process on its own. If the temperature rises above 38°C, doctors usually recommend taking a fever reducer or other medication.

There are many examples of criteria around us: blood pressure, weight, vehicle speed, time... Each of these means something and calls for some kind of response on our part. If your weight is above normal, it means you should pay more attention to your diet and exercise; otherwise, in the short term, you'll need to update your wardrobe, and in the long term, you'll have to consult doctors. If you're speeding, you either need to slow down or be ready to pay a fine. You can't change a train departure or flight time, but you can try to make it to boarding on time.

In our projects, it is equally necessary to ensure that every action related to achieving a result has a Criterion that allows us to understand what is happening: Is everything going according to plan? Is there growth? Or is there a decline?

Therefore, we need to try to define Criteria for each algorithm that will allow us to objectively and consistently measure progress and respond appropriately depending on the level of the Criteria.

To do this, in the table we filled out earlier, you need to define a Criterion for each step in such a way that any person, regardless of their qualifications, can clearly understand how well a particular step has been performed. In other words, it's necessary to introduce a scale for measuring the level of execution of each step, thereby enabling us to evaluate whether we are experiencing growth or decline.

№	Key actions	Steps	Responsible	Criterias	
1	Creating (or acquiring) a product or service:				
1-1	1. Defining the green coffee supplier	1. Establishing contact with suppliers 2. Receiving information about stock availability 3. Negotiating price and delivery terms	The technologist is responsible for preparing the information, while the director approves it.	Supplier Database Coffee Variety Price Quantity Order to Accounting	
1-2	2. Purchasing and delivering green coffee	1. Receiving the invoice 2. Payment 3. Delivery	The accountant is responsible for receiving and paying the invoice, while the logistics manager is responsible for the delivery of raw materials.	Invoice Payment Order Quantity of Green Coffee in Stock According to Invoice	
1-3	3. Roasting and packaging the coffee	1. Roasting a sample 2. Roasting a batch 3. Degassing and packaging	The technologist is responsible for the entire cycle.	Roasting Profile Quantity of Roasted Coffee Quantity of Packaged Coffee	
1-4	4. Moving the coffee to the finished goods warehouse	1. Preparing the invoice 2. Moving the product to the warehouse	The technologist prepares the product and the delivery note. The accountant registers the delivery note in the accounting system. The logistics specialist handles the physical movement.	Invoice Posting of Invoice in the Accounting System Roasted Coffee in the Main Warehouse	

Reflective task:

For the product or service you have chosen, write down the Criteria that will allow you to understand the level of execution for each step and action.

_____

_____

_____

_____

_____

_____

_____

_____

_____

_____

_____

Why is it important to define clear criteria when describing algorithms?

Firstly, it is essential that everyone evaluates the situation in the same way to avoid cases where one employee thinks everything is going well, while another believes that things are going badly! This is why it's important that the criteria are OBJECTIVE! Regardless of who is responsible for the process — whether it's the director's relative or an ordinary employee, a long-standing team member or a new hire — the evaluation criteria for results should be clear and transparent for everyone.

Secondly, it's crucial to acknowledge that every person needs to know that they are doing well and succeeding in their work. If the criteria are objective and the employee has sufficient qualifications and resources, they are more likely to be motivated to achieve good results or take corrective actions when things deviate from the plan. To make this possible, the employee must be familiar with the evaluation criteria for their work. Typically, employees are informed about these criteria through their Job Description or through established standards for performing specific tasks.

Thirdly, having objective evaluation criteria ensures that the entire organization assesses progress consistently and understands what is happening. This minimizes conflicts and misunderstandings within the team.

Fourthly, when building an organizational structure, we can align the criteria of both managers and subordinates. This ensures that employees do not perceive following a manager's instructions as a favor but as a direct part of achieving their results. Likewise, managers will be motivated to ensure that every team member performs well, is trained, and has the necessary resources — because the results of each team member contribute to the overall outcome, which influences the manager's performance evaluation. This creates the second key benefit of criteria indicators — **Team alignment** across the entire hierarchy!

INTEGRAL (CONSOLIDATED) CRITERIA

Obviously, the larger the company, the more processes and employees there are, which means more criteria to monitor! So, how can this be managed? To address this challenge, there is a practice of combining multiple criteria into a single **Integral (Consolidated) Criterion**.

For example, in the sales department, the company's manager doesn't need to monitor the sales performance of each employee or each client on a daily or weekly basis. In such cases, integral criteria — which are created by combining individual (linear) criteria — come to the rescue!

This means that, at the initial level, the manager only needs to review the total sales volume of the team. If any discrepancies or issues are identified, the manager can decompose the consolidated criterion and analyze the performance at the level of individual products, employees, or clients.

LEVEL OF DEVIATION FROM CRITERIA

An important aspect to consider is the approach to evaluating potential deviations from the criteria. What should be done if sales for a week are lower than the previous week? And by how much must they be lower for the manager to "sound the alarm"? (A special question: What does "sounding the alarm" mean in your case?)

The answer to this question is closely related to planning activities. Typically, each department of a company creates a plan (budget) for a reporting period: a year, a quarter, a month, etc. It is important that the plans of all departments are aligned. Otherwise, for example, you may plan to sell something, but you might not have enough resources to produce or purchase the necessary products or services.

So, you have a plan and the actual performance. It's important to define in advance what constitutes an acceptable deviation from the plan. If the results fall within the acceptable deviation range, there's no need to delve into details. However, if the trend persists or the result exceeds the acceptable deviation, then it's time to move to a more detailed level.

From that point onward, each employee or manager at any level can compare the current results with the planned figures and take appropriate actions based on the comparison.

FOOD FOR THOUGHT

During my time working in international companies, I was involved in the sales planning process. Every year, at the beginning of the fourth quarter, we would create a detailed plan for the following year and a forecast for the next three years. Then, after the first quarter, we would conduct a review of the results and adjust the sales plan for the current year, as well as revise the forecast for the next three years. Similar revisions took place at the end of the second and third quarters. At the same time, as the revision at the end of the third quarter, we would present the detailed sales plan for the following year.

When planning our sales, we worked with several possible scenarios: at least two − an optimistic and a pessimistic (conservative) scenario. Both plans were presented to the company's management, which typically approved the conservative plan as the official one, and used it for the global company's indicators. For internal communication, we typically used the optimistic plan, which was slightly higher than the conservative one. It is important to understand that bonuses and rewards started to be calculated based on achieving the conservative plan, thus ensuring proper motivation for every team member. Subsequently, when evaluating results, if the performance was lower than the optimistic plan but higher than the conservative one, we considered it satisfactory.

DEFINITION OF QUALITY CRITERIA

What about processes that, at first glance, do not have clear criteria? With weight, quantity, revenue, costs, speed, and other measurable indicators, it's clear. But what if we need to measure customer satisfaction with a product or service? Or how satisfied the company's staff is with their working conditions or their attitude towards new innovations? In other words, when we need to measure qualitative, not quantitative, indicators. This is where subjective evaluation comes in — a scale that we conventionally perceive as the level at which we assess our progress.

For example, suppose you have introduced a new menu in your establishment, and you truly need to assess customer satisfaction. Then I recommend the following approach: based on the outlined algorithms, we ask customers to rate the product or service or its features on a scale from 1 to 5. By understanding in detail each action and step related to a particular evaluation, you can further break down what exactly caused the customer's dissatisfaction and led to a decrease in the overall satisfaction rating.

As an example, for a restaurant, you can print a postcard with several questions and issue it along with the bill:

Evaluate your impressions of visiting our establishment on a scale from 1 to 5, where 1 means you did not like it at all and 5 means you liked it very much.

1. **What dishes did you order?** _____

2. **Rate your impressions of the presentation of the dishes on a scale from 1 to 5, where 1 means you did not like it at all and 5 means you liked it very much.**

3. **Rate how much you liked the taste of the dishes on a scale from 1 to 5, where 1 means you did not like it at all and 5 means you liked it very much.**

4. **...**

In the end, the owner or manager receives feedback, based on which they can make decisions aimed at improving guest satisfaction. It's also important that if you regularly conduct such assessments, you can track their increase or decrease, which gives you grounds to understand the success of your decisions or the need to implement other measures.

Reflective task:

Do you use Integral Criteria? If yes, what are they and how do you perform their decomposition?

What level of deviation from the defined criteria is unacceptable for you?

Do you have an action plan in case of deviations greater than the acceptable level?

What qualitative indicators could be relevant for you? Choose one at your discretion and create a list of questions to evaluate it.

The First Leg of the Tabouret Principle: the System — Monitoring

Monitoring (from latin, one that warns, overseer, from monēre — to warn) — to watch, keep track of, or check, usually for a special purpose.

In a broad sense, monitoring is the process of continuous or regular (periodic) collection of information about the state of certain parameters of an object or subject of observation (monitoring). The goal of monitoring can be to accumulate information for further analysis and decision-making.

If you can confidently answer "yes" to the statements below, it means that this component of successful work is, to some extent, implemented in your project:

· Each employee can independently see and assess the parameters of their work on a daily basis.

· For each criterion, an acceptable level of deviation from the norm is agreed upon.

· The project collects criteria on a regular basis, with subsequent summary reports based on the week, month, quarter, half-year, or year.

· Each employee has access to the ability to compare their criteria with previous periods and with other team members.

For the cloud of the LORD was upon the tabernacle by day, and fire
was on it by night, in the sight of all the house of Israel, throughout
all their journeys.
— Exodus 40:38

During their journey through the desert, the Israelites had a specific sign that indicated when to set up camp or when to continue on their way. This sign was the cloud over the Tabernacle or the fire. Notice that different signals were used for day and night. Why? The answer is simple: because they were easier to see! During the day, when the sun was blinding, it was easier for them to orient themselves by the clouds. At night, when it was dark, it was easier for them to orient themselves by the fire! Both the fire and the cloud were visible from a distance, which made setting up camp and moving more efficient and organized.

For the leader of any project, it is extremely important to organize the monitoring of key criteria that would allow tracking the dynamics of various indicators. As a result, this would enable the leader to make the right, well-considered decisions. It is also crucial to set up monitoring in such a way that the information arrives on time, allowing for a quick response!

Let's take the example of project revenue. How often should it be monitored? Should you do daily analysis and make decisions? Weekly? Monthly?

If you do an analysis once a month, unfortunately, you must acknowledge that by the end of the reporting month, you won't be able to influence anything. All your decisions and changes will only affect, at best, the next month!

If you do an analysis every day, first of all, you will spend a considerable amount of time on this process, and secondly, your decisions often won't provide significant results due to the consumption cycle of goods or services, inertia in implementing changes, or the cyclical nature of operations (e.g., weekly routes for sales agents).

Therefore, the most optimal period for revenue analysis is weekly. On one hand, you spend time analyzing and agreeing on changes (action plan) only once a week, and on the other hand, since there are at least four full weeks in a month, you can influence the organization of work and the results of the month at least four times.

FOOD FOR THOUGHT:

At the beginning of my career as a sales manager, I led a team of over 50 sales agents and managers spread across Ukraine. To monitor their performance, I used daily and weekly reports, which each of them had to submit via fax. According to the accepted standard, each agent had to record not only the sales of the company's products but also the presence of competitors' products on store shelves. As a result, once a week, I spent almost an entire day analyzing and discussing the results with the regional managers.

One time, during a visit from a head office executive, he asked me if I had time to conduct a thorough analysis of the reports I was receiving. I sincerely replied that initially, when there were fewer sales agents, I could go into detail with the numbers and discuss action plans with each one. But as the number of agents increased, I physically couldn't analyze everything and discuss it with each agent. Therefore, I started to selectively focus on the agents whose sales were falling short of the plan.

The executive then asked me how much time our agents were spending filling out such reports. I answered that, besides submitting the order for the products they then passed to the dealer for delivery, the time spent on monitoring competitors' product availability was just a few minutes per visit. He suggested I calculate how much time this was taking daily, weekly, and monthly for one agent. And for the whole team?

When I did the math, I was stunned. If 2-3 minutes per visit was multiplied by 20 visits a day, it came to about 1 hour per day for one agent! That's 5 hours per week or 20-22 hours per month for one agent! In other words, each month, a sales agent spent almost two and a half working days filling out forms that I couldn't fully process!

As a result of this conversation, we significantly simplified the reporting process, and this gave our team an additional two and a half days to increase sales.

TYPES OF MONITORING APPROACHES BASED ON FREQUENCY:

- Planned or Periodic Monitoring: This type of monitoring is related to providing information based on a pre-agreed schedule. It often includes processes like submitting tax reports, payroll calculations, etc. Examples include daily, weekly, monthly, quarterly, or annual reports.

- Stage-Based Monitoring: For long-term, complex, or change-sensitive projects, a report is provided at the end of each stage to ensure continuity. An example would be monitoring in construction work or manufacturing.

- Unplanned or Selective Monitoring: In cases of significant or systematic deviations from agreed-upon indicators, monitoring outside the agreed agreed-upon schedule can be implemented. Examples include audits or inspections.

From the perspective of the monitoring format, various tools can also be used. Everything is determined by the process and indicators that need to be tracked:

- Reports, briefing notes

- Meetings, personal meetings or visits, video conferences

- Photo reports, before and after photo reports

- Invoices, delivery notes

- Checklists (control lists) ...

Reflective task:

Think about how you could use different monitoring formats for various areas of activity within your project.

_____

_____

_____

_____

_____

If we return to the example describing the process related to the procurement and roasting of green coffee, the monitoring of this process is implemented as follows.

№	Key actions	Steps	Responsible	Criterias	Monitoring
1	Creating (or acquiring) a product or service:				
1-1	1. Defining the green coffee supplier	1. Establishing contact with suppliers 2. Receiving information about stock availability 3. Negotiating price and delivery terms	The technologist is responsible for preparing the information, while the director approves it.	Supplier Database Coffee Variety Price Quantity Order to Accounting	Report note / for each batch Signature on the Report Note / for each batch
1-2	2. Purchasing and delivering green coffee	1. Receiving the invoice 2. Payment 3. Delivery	The accountant is responsible for receiving and paying the invoice, while the logistics manager is responsible for the delivery of raw materials.	Invoice Payment Order Quantity of Green Coffee in Stock According to Invoice	Invoice / for each batch Payment order Goods receipt note / for each batch Certificate of quality / for each batch
1-3	3. Roasting and packaging the coffee	1. Roasting a sample 2. Roasting a batch 3. Degassing and packaging	The technologist is responsible for the entire cycle.	Roasting Profile Quantity of Roasted Coffee Quantity of Packaged Coffee	Batch control sheet / for each batch
1-4	4. Moving the coffee to the finished goods warehouse	1. Preparing the invoice 2. Moving the product to the warehouse	The technologist prepares the product and the delivery note. The accountant registers the delivery note in the accounting system. The logistics specialist handles the physical movement.	Invoice Posting of Invoice in the Accounting System Roasted Coffee in the Main Warehouse	Invoice / for each batch Entry in accounting system / for each batch Inventory / monthly

Leaders often place charts with several key criteria (such as revenue, number of clients, etc.) in the most public areas of the office (e.g., entrance area, kitchen area) and regularly update the data. This approach helps achieve at least the following goals:

- Employees understand the company's priorities and become mobilized to achieve them!

- It encourages not only those directly involved in sales but also employees from other departments. This leads to better coordination and interaction between departments!

- When the information is visible to everyone, it's immediately clear who the leader is and who is lagging behind. Most people don't want to be behind! This creates healthy competition within the team — a desire to be the best, to be successful, to earn praise and recognition, which becomes a powerful motivator!

- Similarly, comparing results with previous periods works in the same way. Organizing monitoring this way not only provides visibility for employees from different departments (similar to how the cloud and pillar of fire were visible to the entire Israeli camp) but also plays a significant role in motivating the team, which we will discuss in the next section.

Reflective task:

For the product or service you have chosen, outline specific monitoring tools for the criteria that will allow you to track the progress of each action and step.

Key conclusions of the section The First Leg of the Tabouret Principle: the System

The First leg of the Tabouret principle represents the System. If your project involves repetitive processes, the system is crucial for the successful implementation of the project! There are 3 elements whose presence indicates that you have implemented a System in your processes:

1. **Algorithms** — a detailed, step-by-step, unambiguous description of all processes.

2. **Criteria** — an objective and agreed-upon definition for evaluating the state or progress of the Algorithms.

3. **Monitoring** — easy and timely access to control the Criteria.

Reflective task:

Review the materials in the section "The First Leg of The Tabouret Principle: The System."

Mark (underline, highlight with a marker, make notes on the margins, etc.) the places that you think are important to share with your team. Plan where and how you can present these to them.

Based on your understanding of the current state of affairs in the project, assess the presence of the System in each department. Invite responsible employees and agree on goals together, creating a plan for implementation.

The Second Leg of the Tabouret Principle: the Team and the Partners

And God said, Let us make man in our image, after our likeness: and let them have dominion over the fish of the sea, and over the fowl of the air, and over the cattle, and over all the earth, and over every creeping thing that creepeth upon the earth. So God created man in his own image, in the image of God created He him; male and female created He them.
— Genesis 1:26-27

The next stage of creation was the creation of man "in Our image and after Our likeness." Notice that immediately, both man and woman were created! By creating both man and woman, the Lord created the first TEAM! Moreover, God Himself became their PARTNER, as the team had specific tasks related to the stewardship of the earth, which they could only carry out in cooperation with God!

And the LORD God took the man, and put him into the garden of Eden to dress it and to keep it.
— Genesis 2:15

As an example of partnership, let's look at growing crops: a person can choose where to plant the seeds, but it is God who makes them grow! And this is our second leg – **TEAM** and **PARTNERS**. Your employees and partners are a crucial component of your project's success.

Team — a number of persons associated together in work or activity, a group on one side (as in football or a debate).

Partners — one associated with another, especially in an action; a person with whom one shares an intimate relationship; a member of a partnership, especially in a business.

There is a saying that if you want something done well, do it yourself. And indeed, each of us has probably encountered the situation where, as long as we do something ourselves, we are satisfied with the result. But as soon as we entrust the task to someone else, the results immediately become, to put it mildly, less satisfying. At first glance, this seems true. However... each of us has only two hands, two legs, and no eyes on the back of our heads. Each of us has very limited capabilities on our own. Therefore, if you want to accomplish something on a larger scale, there is no alternative to creating a team!

If you are familiar with the First Leg of the Tabouret (the System) and have completed the task, it will be easier for you to proceed with the team aspect. Why do I emphasize this? Because first comes the system, and then the team! Agree, even if you put the most talented hamster in a wheel, it will just run in circles! You need to think through the system and create the conditions to leverage the talents and abilities of each team member with the highest Efficiency!

Efficiency — productive of desired effects; capable of producing desired results with little or no waste (as of time or materials).

With a well-thought-out system in place, the team is what can allow you to grow and scale!

> *Two are better than one; because they have a good reward for their labour. For if they fall, the one will lift up his fellow: but woe to him that is alone when he falleth; for he hath not another to help him up. Again, if two lie together, then they have heat: but how can one be warm alone? And if one prevail against him, two shall withstand him; and a threefold cord is not quickly broken.*
> — *Ecclesiastes 4:9-12*

Even though the first team, in the form of Adam and Eve, stumbled, resulting in the fall of man, we can still learn important lessons from how it was organized and how it functioned.

1. KNOWING

The first thing to pay attention to is that in the first team, both its members — the man and the woman — were created in the image and likeness of God! Being made in the image and likeness of God, a person had certain knowledge and abilities necessary to accomplish the tasks set before the team. I call this quality **KNOWING**. In other words, in order to handle various tasks, a person must first have certain knowledge and abilities!

So God created man in his own image, in the image of God created
he him; male and female created he them.
— Genesis 1:26-27

2. CAPABLE OR BEING ABLE

KNOWING is the potential. However, it is important to be able to use this potential as effectively as possible. And here we move on to another crucial quality that has practical application — **CAPABILITY or TO BE ABLE**. You may be knowing, but not having the practical skills to apply that knowledge. To be useful, one must be able to practically use knowledge to achieve the desired result. The person created by the Lord was so gifted that they were able to give names to all the animals and birds. It is important to understand that giving a name is not just about coming up with a word. It means understanding the essence and identifying the main point. I believe that it was then that animals and birds, which later became known as domesticated, were distinguished. And to distinguish them, one had to understand and see their application!

And out of the ground the LORD God formed every beast of the
field, and every fowl of the air; and brought them unto Adam to see
what he would call them: and whatsoever Adam called every living
creature, that was the name thereof. And Adam gave names to all
cattle, and to the fowl of the air, and to every beast of the field; but
for Adam there was not found an help meet for him.
— Genesis 2:19-20

· Alex Marchuk ·

3. WANTING OR MOTIVATION

The Lord does not limit Himself to ensuring that a person knows and is skilled! We see that when the Lord gives the person the command regarding tasting the fruits, He does not just instruct them, but also gives them the incentive to obey! In other words, He motivates them. I call this quality — **WANTING or MOTIVATION!**

> And the LORD God commanded the man, saying, Of every tree of the garden thou mayest freely eat: But of the tree of the knowledge of good and evil, thou shalt not eat of it: for in the day that thou eatest thereof thou shalt surely die.
> — Genesis 2:16-17

4. EXECUTING

Unfortunately, **KNOWING, BEING ABLE** and **WANTING** are not enough for things to move forward! It is important to — EXECUTE!

FOOD FOR THOUGHT

When I conducted seminars on "The Tabouret Principle", I often heard roughly the same question from the audience: "If a person knows, is skilled, and wants to, how is it possible that they don't execute?" Considering that some participants at the seminars weren't very familiar with the Bible or the story of Adam and Eve, I would provide the following example to the audience: "Tell me, do you know that exercise is good for your health?" Generally, everyone would agree. "Great," I would continue, "now, raise your hands if you know how to do an exercise?" Usually, everyone would raise their hands. "Wonderful, now tell me, who wants to be healthy?" Again, everyone raised their hands. "Super," I would say, "then who did exercise today?" Typically, from an audience of 25-50 people, only a few hands would be raised.

This is precisely why, even though a person knew, was skilled, and wanted to, they did not act as they should have, which led to the fall and created a barrier between the Holy Righteous Creator and His creation—the human being!

And when the woman saw that the tree was good for food, and that it was pleasant to the eyes, and a tree to be desired to make one wise, she took of the fruit thereof, and did eat, and gave also unto her husband with her; and he did eat. And the eyes of them both were opened, and they knew that they were naked; and they sewed fig leaves together, and made themselves aprons.
— Genesis 3:6-7

This is why later the atoning sacrifice of Jesus Christ was needed to remove the obstacle of sin from our relationship with the Heavenly Father! Every time we fail to do what we know, able to do, and want to do, consequences arise.

For if by one man's offence death reigned by one; much more they which receive abundance of grace and of the gift of righteousness shall reign in life by one, Jesus Christ. Therefore as by the offence of one judgment came upon all men to condemnation; even so by the righteousness of one the free gift came upon all men unto justification of life. For as by one man's disobedience many were made sinners, so by the obedience of one shall many be made righteous.
— Romans 5:17-19

Every project manager must understand that the First Leg of **The Tabouret Principle** — the SYSTEM — is crucial for either preventing non-execution or minimizing the consequences of something being done improperly!

And now let's look at the **PARTNERS**.

And Moses said unto God, Who am I, that I should go unto Pharaoh, and that I should bring forth the children of Israel out of Egypt? And he said, Certainly I will be with thee; and this shall be a token unto thee, that I have sent thee: When thou hast brought forth the people out of Egypt, ye shall serve God upon this mountain.
— Exodus 3:11-12

Fear thou not; for I am with thee: be not dismayed; for I am thy God: I will strengthen thee; yea, I will help thee; yea, I will uphold thee with the right hand of my righteousness.
— Isaiha 41:10

Whatever you are engaged in, an essential component of your success is your **PARTNERS**: co-founders, suppliers, contractors, clients... A partner can be any company, organization, or individual with whom you interact but over whom you have no direct control! While your employees and team members are within your direct sphere of influence — where you can apply both incentives and penalties, including termination — the situation with partners is different! You need to establish truly mutually beneficial terms of cooperation that will create a win-win outcome for both you and your partner!

FOOD FOR THOUGHT

When discussing the interaction between two parties, the following relationship scenarios are typically identified:

Lose-Lose

This scenario occurs when neither party is willing to compromise or meet the other halfway, resulting in missed opportunities for both sides. For example, this could happen in a buyer-seller relationship where neither party is willing to give ground. While both parties may feel they are protecting their own interests, there's still a chance they might reach a better agreement in the future.

Win-Lose

In my opinion, this is the worst possible scenario. It usually happens when one party holds more leverage than the other and exploits this imbalance, often manipulatively. On one hand, the losing party experiences losses or missed profits, which is unpleasant. However, the greater damage comes from the resentment it breeds in the losing party, creating a desire for revenge. As a result, building trust and fostering future cooperation becomes difficult. The situation can be corrected if the winning party acknowledges its past mistakes and offers some form of concession to the losing party as a way of "making amends" for previous losses.

Win-Win

This is the most desirable and stable scenario. It ensures that both parties benefit over time and lays the foundation for trusting, long-term relationships. Such relationships can even lead to joint ventures or business partnerships. Furthermore, from a ministry perspective, this type of scenario opens hearts and creates opportunities to discuss not only business matters but also personal ones — including faith and the Gospel.

One of the most striking examples of partnership with God is the relationship between the Lord and Abraham. This relationship can be described through the following three points:

1. BENEFIT TODAY

Abraham believed God and was obedient to Him. Just imagine the reaction of your loved ones if one day you came home and shared that God had spoken to you and commanded you to move to another place. When asked, "Where?" — you have no answer! But you are certain that you need to move.

> *Now the LORD had said unto Abram, Get thee out of thy country, and from thy kindred, and from thy father's house, unto a land that I will shew thee: And I will make of thee a great nation, and I will bless thee, and make thy name great; and thou shalt be a blessing: And I will bless them that bless thee, and curse him that curseth thee: and in thee shall all families of the earth be blessed. So Abram departed, as the LORD had spoken unto him; and Lot went with him: and Abram was seventy and five years old when he departed out of Haran.*
> — *Genesis 12:1-4*

For His part, God blessed Abraham with everything he needed throughout his life and protected him.

> *And Abram was very rich in cattle, in silver, and in gold.*
> — *Genesis 13:2*

> *And it came to pass at that time, that Abimelech and Phichol the chief captain of his host spake unto Abraham, saying, God is with thee in all that thou doest:*
> — *Genesis 21:22*

> *And the LORD hath blessed my master greatly; and he is become great: and he hath given him flocks, and herds, and silver, and gold, and menservants, and maidservants, and camels, and asses.*
> — *Genesis 24:35*

2. STABILITY

Just imagine — from the moment Abraham heard God's words about his inheritance until the birth of a son from Sarah, 25 years passed! Throughout that time, Abraham remained faithful to the covenant with God and obedient to Him. Perhaps he had thoughts about returning to Haran, to his relatives, where there was some stability and safety. But even if such thoughts arose, Abraham did not give in to them! On the other hand, God constantly cared for Abraham. Whenever Abraham found himself in difficult situations, the Lord was always there, protecting and supporting him!

So Abram departed, as the LORD had spoken unto him; and Lot went with him: and Abram was seventy and five years old when he departed out of Haran.

And Abraham was an hundred years old, when his son Isaac was born unto him.
— Genesis 12:4; 21:5

And the LORD plagued Pharaoh and his house with great plagues because of Sarai Abram's wife. And Pharaoh called Abram, and said, What is this that thou hast done unto me? why didst thou not tell me that she was thy wife? Why saidst thou, She is my sister? so I might have taken her to me to wife: now therefore behold thy wife, take her, and go thy way. And Pharaoh commanded his men concerning him: and they sent him away, and his wife, and all that he had.
— Genesis 12:17-20

But God came to Abimelech in a dream by night, and said to him, Behold, thou art but a dead man, for the woman which thou hast taken; for she is a man's wife. But Abimelech had not come near her: and he said, Lord, wilt thou slay also a righteous nation? Said he not unto me, She is my sister? and she, even she herself said, He is my brother: in the integrity of my heart and innocency of my hands have I done this. And God said unto him in a dream, Yea, I know that thou didst this in the integrity of thy heart; for I also withheld thee from sinning against me: therefore suffered I thee not to touch her. Now therefore restore the man his wife; for he is a prophet, and he shall pray for thee, and thou shalt live: and if thou restore her not, know thou that thou shalt surely die, thou, and all that are thine.
— Genesis 20:3-7

3. PERSPECTIVE

Perspective is important for partnership. Agree, if you expect long-term relationships, you will be much more open to finding mutually beneficial solutions than if you're dealing with a short-term encounter or one-time cooperation. In the second case, you simply state your terms, and it doesn't matter whether the other party agrees with them or not. What's more important for you are those who will walk with you for a long time! Knowing Abraham's deepest desires, the Lord supported his faith and inspired him. Even though Abraham (at Sarah's initiative!) tried to solve the issue of an heir in his own way, the Lord remained faithful to His promises and eventually fulfilled them! In turn, because of his faith, Abraham was able to endure the trial regarding God's command to sacrifice his son, was called "God's friend" and truly became the patriarch of all believers.

> *And the LORD said unto Abram, after that Lot was separated from him, Lift up now thine eyes, and look from the place where thou art northward, and southward, and eastward, and westward: For all the land which thou seest, to thee will I give it, and to thy seed for ever. And I will make thy seed as the dust of the earth: so that if a man can number the dust of the earth, then shall thy seed also be numbered.*
> — *Genesis 13:14-16*

> *And the angel of the LORD called unto Abraham out of heaven the second time, And said, By myself have I sworn, saith the LORD, for because thou hast done this thing, and hast not withheld thy son, thine only son: That in blessing I will bless thee, and in multiplying I will multiply thy seed as the stars of the heaven, and as the sand which is upon the sea shore; and thy seed shall possess the gate of his enemies; And in thy seed shall all the nations of the earth be blessed; because thou hast obeyed my voice.*
> — *Genesis 22:15-18*

> *Even as Abraham believed God, and it was accounted to him for righteousness. Know ye therefore that they which are of faith, the same are the children of Abraham. And the scripture, foreseeing that God would justify the heathen through faith, preached before the gospel unto Abraham, saying, In thee shall all nations be blessed.*
> — *Galatians 3:6-8*

By faith Abraham, when he was tried, offered up Isaac: and he that had received the promises offered up his only begotten son, Of whom it was said, That in Isaac shall thy seed be called: Accounting that God was able to raise him up, even from the dead; from whence also he received him in a figure.
— *Hebrews 11:17-19*

In general, we have described the qualities that a **TEAM** and **PARTNERS** should have in order for projects to achieve their goals. Next, we will break down these qualities in detail.

The Second Leg of the Tabouret Principle: the Team — Knowing

Knowledge — the fact or condition of knowing something with familiarity gained through experience or association.

If you can confidently answer "yes" to the statements below, it means that this component of successful work is, to some extent, implemented in your project:

- The First Leg of the Tabouret Principle has been implemented in your project.

- Consolidated information (on the website or in a printed brochure) about the company/organization, its products/services, key milestones, and achievements is available. Moreover, this information is regularly updated.

- For each position according to the organizational chart, informational printed, audio, and video materials that describe all the details of successfully executing tasks within that position are available. Additionally, this information is regularly updated.

- For key positions/areas of activity, an "Achievements" book has been implemented, which records all the most effective practices and accomplishments within that position/area of activity. Furthermore, this information is regularly updated.

- A personal development plan for employees (or periodic assessments) exists, within which they can receive feedback and recommendations on areas where they can deepen their knowledge.

(As) an archer that woundeth all, So is he that hireth a fool and he
that hireth them that pass by.
— Proverbs 26:10 (American Standard Bible)

KNOWING begins with the team selection process — **HIRING**. Everyone knows the old fable about the swan, the crayfish, and the pike. They tried to move the cart. They pulled together, but no matter how hard they tried, they couldn't move it! One pulled upwards, another backed up, and the third pulled forward!

How to correctly organize the team selection process? Let's turn to the Bible.

In the Book of Exodus, there is a description of a situation related to the establishment of the "organizational structure" in Israel. Up until this point, Moses was the only person making decisions on various disputes. As a result, Moses was busy from morning until late evening. This exhausted both him and the people: while Moses was judging, the people were standing in line waiting for him. Moreover, while he was occupied with resolving claims, he couldn't dedicate time to receiving the vision from God regarding where to lead the people! He didn't have a map, nor a GPS navigator. The final destination, "the land flowing with milk and honey, the land of the Canaanites, Hittites, Amorites, Perizzites, Hivites, and Jebusites" looked quite vague. Therefore, it was important for Moses to receive understanding from the Lord about where to lead the people.

And when Moses' father-in-law saw what he was doing, he gave him invaluable advice that helped him resolve many issues:

> *Hearken now unto my voice, I will give thee counsel, and God be with thee: be thou for the people to God-ward, and bring thou the causes unto God: and thou shalt teach them the statutes and the laws, and shalt show them the way wherein they must walk, and the work that they must do. Moreover thou shalt provide out of all the people able men, such as fear God, men of truth, hating unjust gain; and place such over them, to be rulers of thousands, rulers of hundreds, rulers of fifties, and rulers of tens: and let them judge the people at all seasons: and it shall be, that every great matter they shall bring unto thee, but every small matter they shall judge themselves: so shall it be easier for thyself, and they shall bear (the burden) with thee.*
> *— Exodus 18:19-22*

In this recommendation, I would like to highlight a few points:

1. The first requirement in the list is the word "capable." This emphasizes that each person has certain gifts and talents to engage in a particular task. How do we understand that a person has abilities? By their fruits! Jesus said in the Sermon on the Mount:

> *Beware of false prophets, who come to you in sheep's clothing, but inwardly are ravening wolves. By their fruits ye shall know them. Do (men) gather grapes of thorns, or figs of thistles? Even so every good tree bringeth forth good fruit; but the corrupt tree bringeth forth evil*

fruit. A good tree cannot bring forth evil fruit, neither can a corrupt tree bring forth good fruit. Every tree that bringeth not forth good fruit is hewn down, and cast into the fire. Therefore by their fruits ye shall know them.
— Matthew 7:15-20

That is, if a person has previously engaged in similar activities, has experience, and has had good results (fruits), it is likely that they have the abilities for this activity.

2. After abilities, qualities related to value concepts are separately highlighted.

    God-fearing people are those who know that even if no one around them ever sees or finds out, there is One from whom they cannot hide! Everything we think, say, and do is open to our Heavenly Father. And if this is significant for a person, it means they have additional reasons to act correctly in various situations, orienting themselves on God's commandments rather than human approval.

    Men of Truth has several translations: reliable, constant, faithful. Agree, it is important for every leader that the team includes people who, so to speak, are with you "to the end," not just for this moment and for the paycheck, but also for ideological reasons!

    Hating unjust gain means they make fair decisions based on the well-being of the project, not the desire for personal profit.

3. The next point is that the organizational structure is built from top to bottom: first, the leaders of thousands are selected, then the people who are accountable to them, and so on. Why is this the case? One of the key reasons is efficiency. If people know and trust each other, there is no need to spend extra time double-checking each other's decisions. This way, relatively high decision-making speed is achieved within the organization.

4. And finally, the last management link is the "decenary" or "line manager," who oversees ten people. Therefore, if a manager has more than ten subordinates, he could be overloaded. If there are fewer, he may have time to address other tasks as well.

FOOD FOR THOUGHT

A well-known expert in management and organizational development, Iczhak Calderon Adizes, developed a management and consulting methodology that describes four essential roles needed for the successful management of any organization. Each role performs specific functions, and a harmonious combination of all four roles in an organization enables the company to develop successfully:

Producer (P), responsible for performing tasks and achieving results directly related to your product or service.

Administrator (A), ensuring systematization, order, and control of processes, including accounting and reporting.

Entrepreneur (E), focused on innovation, development, and vision of the future, with an emphasis on marketing and sales.

Integrator (I), facilitating the creation of synergy and effective interaction within the team or between executive leadership.

Complementarity (from English complement — to complement) refers to mutual correspondence; the ability of elements within a structure to complement each other. This can be achieved when the organization effectively combines these roles, compensating for weaknesses in one function by leveraging the strengths of others. This allows for the creation of flexible, adaptive, and resilient structures capable of successfully handling both internal and external challenges.

The team selection process is based on job descriptions. These descriptions define the skills a candidate should have in a particular field and the other qualities they need to possess. Based on the job description for each position within the organizational structure, it is necessary to create an "Ideal Candidate Profile" (ICP) — a description of the characteristics of a person who would best handle the responsibilities outlined in the job description. I generally divide the ICP into three parts: **spirit**, **soul**, and **body:**

- The spirit is connected to worldview and values.

- The soul is linked to the mind (education), character (traits), and will (experience and skills).

- The body relates both to the physical body itself (appearance, speech, physical condition) and to the possession of specific resources like a car or a computer (which may be a requirement for certain positions).

From a practical standpoint, it is recommended to create the Ideal Candidate Profile (ICP) by simply describing the profile of people who currently hold the position and are successfully fulfilling their duties. As an example, consider the ICP for the position of Senior Barista at one of the coffee shops:

Ideal Candidate Profile:	
Principles and Values:	Shares the company's mission, vision, and values.
Knowledge, Skills, Experience, Personal Qualities:	Experience in a customer-facing role; enthusiasm, openness to learning, honesty, responsibility, discipline, and strong communication skills.
Physical Requirements:	25–40 years old, male or female, with clear speech and no bad habits.

Note that the company did not emphasize coffee-making skills. The company had a well-established training system, allowing even someone without experience to understand coffee and prepare decent drinks within a few days. The key quality valued for this position was communicability.

FOOD FOR THOUGHT

Once, I came across the Ideal Candidate Profile (ICP) for the position of store manager at a well-known retail chain. I noticed that one of the criteria listed, word for word, was: "A divorced woman with one or more children, living separately." At first glance, this seemed quite shocking. I had the opportunity to speak with one of the company's managers and ask about this parameter. He responded with something like this: "We didn't invent anything. We simply described the profile of our most successful managers."

When you think about it, it becomes clear that in such a situation — as described in the profile — a woman would likely have to mobilize herself to the fullest, which could explain why she is able to achieve outstanding results.

Reflective task:

For a selected position, create an Ideal Candidate Profile (ICP) based on the job description. I recommend drawing from examples of people you know (team members) who have successfully handled their responsibilities.

After selecting a team member, it is essential to introduce them to the matter at hand — **INTRODUCTION**. This is the second stage of KNOWING.

Train up a child in the way he should go: and when he is old, he will not depart from it.
— Proverbs 22:6

Even if a candidate has previous experience in the field, the requirements and work standards at their old job may differ significantly from those followed in your organization. It is clear that the quicker a new team member becomes familiar with the workflow, the sooner they will begin to deliver results! To achieve this, you must familiarize them with the standards, rules, and traditions adopted within your organization. In other words, we need to help them effectively absorb the information and quickly adapt to the new environment!

Although everyone has almost unlimited access to the internet and "Google and artificial intelligence know everything," for each position, it is important to prepare an information package that provides the necessary theoretical foundation for successfully completing tasks. If an employee is interested in working with you, they can, of course, find all the necessary information online themselves. However, they will spend much more time doing so, and the information will not be properly organized. What should be prioritized? What works better in this organization and these conditions, and what works worse? Only you have this information and can structure it properly, ensuring it is presented effectively to the new employee.

Thus, not only will you create the conditions for efficient onboarding, but you will also provide them with an information base they can return to as needed in the future.

What could this be and how might it look? I recommend considering the following tools:

- **Company Information:** An overview of the company, its products/services, management, organizational chart, target audience, and clients.

- **Description of Standards:** Clear guidelines and standards for performing various tasks or procedures within the company.

- **Achievement Book:** A collection of examples where employees of the company have excelled, showcasing their best performances or successes.

- **Recommendations:** A curated list of books, films, audio, or video materials that are helpful for the role, including online resources.

These resources would form the foundation of an onboarding package that provides a comprehensive understanding of the organization and its practices, helping the new team member integrate more effectively and quickly.

FOOD FOR THOUGHT

At one point, while working at an international company, my team and I successfully launched a corporate quarterly magazine. In this magazine, there were several sections, one of which was dedicated to achievements in the sales department. Sales teams working across Ukraine regularly sent in their stories, and being featured in the magazine not only provided an opportunity to share the best solutions and experiences but also served as a form of recognition for their achievements, which in turn acted as motivation!

Reflective task:

For the chosen position, based on the available job description, select the informational and training materials that you think are necessary for the successful performance of the duties.

The third stage of KNOWING is related to development — **Individual Development Plan!**

Give instruction to a wise man, and he will be yet wiser: teach a just man, and he will increase in learning.
— Proverbs 9:9

But grow in grace, and in the knowledge of our Lord and Saviour Jesus Christ. To him be glory both now and for ever. Amen.
— 2 Peter 3:18

The Word of God calls each of us to constantly develop and grow!

The market doesn't stand still. Consumers and their needs change. Technologies do as well. And, of course, competitors are also moving forward. We need to adapt to new requirements and, ideally, stay several steps ahead of our competitors. Therefore, it's important for all the informational base and knowledge accumulated in the company to be regularly reviewed and updated to align with the market situation!

To implement this, it's essential, on one hand, to introduce an **Individual Development Program** for employees, which encourages self-growth, and on the other hand, to create and maintain an atmosphere in the organization that is charged with renewal and improvement!

FOOD FOR THOUGHT

Kaizen (from Japanese: 改善, meaning "continuous improvement" or "improvement for the better") is a Japanese philosophy or practice that focuses on the continuous improvement of production processes, development, auxiliary business processes, management, and all aspects of an organization's life.

"Kaizen" in business refers to continuous improvement, starting from production and extending to senior management, from the director to the ordinary worker. By improving standardized actions and processes, the goal of Kaizen is to achieve production without waste, also known as "Lean Manufacturing."

The Kaizen approach was first applied in several Japanese companies (including Toyota) during the post-World War II recovery period, and since then, it has spread worldwide and has become synonymous with continuous improvement in work methods and personal efficiency, making it a sort of business philosophy.

Here, I share with you an example of how the Individual Development Plan (IDP) form looks in one of the companies that I was related to. The form is filled out every year based on achievements from the past year and goals for the next year. Throughout the year, the progress is evaluated quarterly or, at a minimum, at the end of the semester, and adjustments are made if necessary. Regarding the procedure for filling out the form, the employee first performs a self-assessment and fills out their part. Then, they submit it to their direct supervisor, who adds their comments. The completed form is discussed and agreed upon during a one-on-one meeting.

Individual Development Plan		
Name:	**Date:**	
Date of start at the company	**Position**	**Previous position**
	Self assessment	**Manager's feedback**
Achievements for the reporting period		
Values	(1) Knows and strives to follow; (2) Consistently follows on a regular basis; (3) Demonstrates an example for others to follow	
Truthfulness and sincerity		
Awareness and respect		
Proactivity and enthusiasm		
Knowledge/ Skills	(1) Understands the theoretical foundation and has limited practical skills; (2) Understands the theory and possesses the necessary practical skills; (3) Takes initiative and applies acquired knowledge/skills to promote the company's culture and vision	
Coffee		
Equiment		
Sales and Negotiations		
Analysis and Administration		
Goals/ Plans		
Personal development		
Skills and Qualities development		
Career development		
	Signature	Signature

Reflective task:

Based on the information read, create a list of actions/steps that, in your opinion, will contribute to the development and updating of the knowledge base and the further improvement of various processes within the organization.

The Second Leg of the Tabouret Principle: the Team — Being able

BEING ABLE or CAPABLE (SKILLS) — the ability to use one's knowledge effectively and readily in execution or performance; dexterity or coordination, especially in the execution of learned physical tasks; a learned power of doing something competently; a developed aptitude or ability.

If you can confidently answer "yes" to the statements below, it means that this component of successful work is, to some extent, implemented in your project:

- The First Leg of the Tabouret Principle (System) is implemented in your project

- You implemented the onboarding process for new employees, where a key element is demonstrating the execution of duties

- You implemented Mentorship

- You have an Employee Individual Development Plan (IDP), where they can receive feedback and recommendations on areas to improve their skills

Go ye therefore, and teach all nations, baptizing them in the name of the Father, and of the Son, and of the Holy Ghost: Teaching them to observe all things whatsoever I have commanded you: and, lo, I am with you always, even unto the end of the world. Amen.
— Matthew 28:19-20

Usually, when reading this passage, which is often referred to as "the Great Commandment of Jesus," people associate the word "teach" based on their experiences in kindergarten, school, or university. That is, there is a teacher who knows more than others, and there are students sitting at desks, diligently taking notes from the instructor. However, the word translated as "teach" is literally translated as "make or acquire disciples."

FOOD FOR THOUGHT

The number of this word in Strong's Concordance is 3100. The original word in Greek is μαΘητεύω (pronounced math-ayt-yoo'-o) — to prepare (or acquire) disciples, to teach, to instruct; to be a disciple.

Moreover, if we recall how Jesus taught the apostles, it was certainly not theoretical! The apostles spent time with Jesus, ate together, traveled together, and saw how Jesus reacted to difficulties and aggression. So, it wasn't only what Jesus said, but also what He did! Add to this the fact that the teaching method underlying modern schools and universities was developed by Jan Amos Comenius around the mid-17th century. Before that, the system of learning primarily functioned on the principle of: master — apprentices, teacher — student. In other words, there was someone with expertise, and students would come to them, often living under the same roof, spending most of their time together. In this process, not only was there a transfer of skills and trade secrets, but also the shaping of character and values.

Regarding the new employee, this means that it's not enough to just provide information about how to properly do something; it's necessary to demonstrate and show visually how certain standards and procedures work, and help them master the skills required for successfully performing their tasks. This can be implemented in several ways.

FOOD FOR THOUGHT

My career in international companies started as a sales representative. It was mid-summer, and very hot. My employer produced chocolate and chocolate candies. On my first day at work, I was given a price list and a printout in English describing the techniques for selling the products. The next day, I was already heading out to one of the districts in Kyiv to sell the company's products! One of my visits has stayed vividly in my memory. I walked into the storeroom and knocked on the store manager's office door. When I entered, I saw two overweight women waving a newspaper at each other instead of using fans. After the introduction, one of the women picked up a bar of chocolate by the corner, which had become so soft due to the heat that right before my eyes, the chocolate started bending toward the table. "What chocolate? Bring some water!" said the store manager. That day, I made about 20 visits, and everywhere I went, the situation was the same. I was very upset that I couldn't sell anything that entire day! So, when, during one of the last visits, I was asked to provide a price list, I was ready to jump to the ceiling with joy, and I eagerly placed a large order for the store. Unfortunately, I later faced delays in payment, returns of expired products, and complaints from the accounting department... I could have avoided many mistakes and losses if I had had the opportunity to undergo training with someone more experienced.

The first method is **Internship**. You can assign the new employee to work alongside an experienced colleague for a period of time (several hours or days). During this time, not only is experience demonstrated and passed on to the newcomer, but when properly organized, this action becomes a powerful motivational tool for the experienced employee as well! By participating in the training of the new employee, the experienced worker is essentially fulfilling the manager's task and, in this way, tests themselves in a new role while gaining the potential for career growth.

Reflective task:

Based on the selected job description, create an internship plan that includes the demonstration of how to perform certain tasks.

The second method is **Mentorship**. After mastering the theory, the employee, together with their direct manager, begins to perform certain tasks. In this process, the manager demonstrates how to perform the tasks for the first few times. This not only shows the company standards but also lays the foundation for future relationships with the employee — the manager demonstrates his expertise, thus earning trust and authority within the team!

Of course, the demonstration at the beginning of skill formation is not the only method! You have a great opportunity to use team meetings to organize various role-playing situations, where some employees act as clients, and others as company employees. After each role-play, a debriefing is conducted, where participants first comment on their actions, and then each observer can provide their feedback. In this way, you give team members the opportunity to practice and create possibilities for sharing experiences.

In fact, it's not necessary to wait for team meetings to organize such role-playing practices. At any convenient moment, the manager can initiate a role-playing exercise even in a one-on-one setting with an employee. Moreover, role-playing learning often creates conditions where people transform into different roles and may reveal more about themselves or show qualities that might not emerge in everyday tasks. By paying attention to the dynamics and behavior of participants in the game, you can form a more comprehensive impression of the skills and qualities of the team members.

FOOD FOR THOUGHT:

Once, I had to conduct a sales skills seminar for over 200 people on the topic of massage equipment. Given that the audience wasn't familiar with me beforehand, some of them were skeptical: "What could they learn from me?" When we moved to the technique of overcoming objections, which consists of four steps, one of which is agreeing with the customer, one participant loudly commented: "How can you agree when your product is called 'Chinese crap'?!"

I invited this person to come up and demonstrate how this technique works in practice. He agreed. Playing the role of a client, with emotions likely stemming from hearing such an objection and not knowing how to respond, he said, "Your massage chairs are just 'Chinese crap'!" I noticed the tension in the audience. If I failed in this challenge, what could I possibly teach them next?

"I agree with you!" The tension in the room only grew. "I thought the same thing before I tried this massage chair! You know, a few years ago, I had a serious car accident, and after that, I could barely sit for a few hours at a time. But when I had my first massage, I felt so much better! And after a few sessions, I noticed the pain was gone, and I felt great, able to work all day without the pain distracting me! Tell me, would you like to feel better?"

My counterpart shrugged, acknowledging that it was a successful response to what seemed like a serious objection. The audience began to applaud us! After the seminar, many participants approached me and thanked me for the demonstration! I stayed in touch with many of them long after the seminar.

Reflective task:

Based on the chosen job description, prepare several scenarios for role-playing exercises to practice certain skills.

Another powerful method for skill development is **Execution of Tasks**. Of course, this should never look like "Go there, I don't know where. Bring that, I don't know what!" The manager needs to carefully define the goals of the task and ensure that, considering the skill level and available resources, the objectives are achievable for the employee! If the employee can complete the tasks and achieve the goals, they will not only improve their skills but also receive an additional boost of motivation! After all, everyone enjoys achieving results and being successful! When you succeed in doing something well, you're happy to do it again and again!

Reflective task:

Based on the selected job description, create a list of tasks that will help develop or strengthen specific skills through task execution.

Another method of skill development used for experienced employees is **Changing Their Area of Activity**. Developing employees' skills through changing their work environment not only promotes their professional and personal growth but also helps the organization adapt to changes, improve overall workflows, and form a strong leadership team. This can be implemented through delegating everyday tasks or by facilitating horizontal movement of employees between departments (for example, a sales department employee undergoes training in the marketing or finance department, a production department employee interns in the marketing or sales department, etc.). In this case, skill development is achieved because the employee faces new tasks that differ from the routine ones. Unlike the familiar environment and tasks, which are often performed automatically, in the new environment, we create conditions where the employee must mobilize and, while acquiring new skills, adapt their existing skills to successfully complete the assigned tasks. Additionally, by mastering new skills, the employee will inevitably transform them through the lens of their experience, potentially generating many interesting ideas and suggestions that could improve work processes and relationships within the team. This approach is often used in the implementation of Kaizen.

FOOD FOR THOUGHT

For the successful implementation of a Change in the Area of Activity, it is essential to pay attention to the following aspects:

1. **Planning:** Prepare specific goals and formulate success criteria for the change in activity.

2. **Support:** Ensure active support from the heads of relevant departments and provide the necessary resources.

3. **Feedback:** Regularly organize feedback and progress evaluations for employees.

4. **Mentorship:** Assign mentors and coaches to support employees during their adaptation to new roles.

Reflective task:

Based on the selected job description, create a list of tasks that will help develop or strengthen certain skills through a change in the area of activity.

It goes without saying that skill development should be tied to a systematic approach to employee development or the Employee **Individual Development Plan (IDP)**. Any employee will be more motivated to perform certain actions if they understand how it will contribute to their personal and career development! If you have completed tasks related to the first leg of The Tabouret Principle — The System — it will be much easier for you to implement the Employee **IDP**. For successful implementation of a systematic approach, the following key points should be considered:

- **Training Needs Analysis:** Conduct an assessment of the current knowledge and skills of employees to identify gaps and determine areas that need development. Evaluate which skills and knowledge will be required for the company in the future to prepare employees for these demands.

- **Development of Training Programs:** Create individual development plans for each employee, considering their current and future needs. Use a combination of learning methods, including training, online courses, workshops, mentoring, and job rotation.

- **Implementation and Execution:** Ensure support from leadership and the HR department for the successful implementation of training programs. Cultivate an awareness among employees about the importance of continuous learning and self-development.

- **Monitoring and Evaluating Results:** Regularly assess employee progress using feedback methods, testing, and evaluation sessions. Make necessary adjustments to training programs based on the data collected to ensure they remain relevant and effective.

- **Reward and Recognition:** Create a reward and recognition system for employees who actively participate in training and demonstrate significant progress. Publicly acknowledging employees' successes will help motivate others to actively engage in learning.

Implementing a systematic approach to employee development requires a well-thought-out strategy and ongoing support, but these efforts pay off in the form of improved productivity, high employee motivation and retention, as well as the company's ability to adapt and thrive in changing conditions.

Reflective task:

Based on the selected job description, create your own version of the employee Individual Development Plan template.

The Second Leg of The Tabouret Principle: the Team — Wanting (Motivation)

Wanting or Motivation (from Latin motus, past participle of movēre to move) — something (such as a need or desire) that causes a person to act.

If you can confidently answer "yes" to the statements below, it means that this component of successful work is, to some extent, implemented in your project:

- You implemented the First Leg of the Tabouret Principle (System)

- You have a clear understanding of motivators, and do you use them on a regular basis

- You have a clear understanding of "hygiene factors," and regularly review them for market relevance

Wherefore, my beloved, as ye have always obeyed, not as in my presence only, but now much more in my absence, work out your own salvation with fear and trembling. For it is God which worketh in you both to will and to do of his good pleasure.
— Philippians 2:12-13

When we think about our Heavenly Father, one of the characteristics that comes to mind is "Almighty"! After all, the Lord created the heavens and everything in them, the earth and everything on it. There's not a single day when we can imagine life without seeing the key role of the Lord, who is the source of all life! Imagine, even our Almighty Heavenly Father doesn't just make us act, turning us into mindless, soulless robots, but He gives us "to will and to do"! For some reason, it's important to God that we want to act, that it is our decision, a manifestation of our choice, faith, and will! In this section, we will talk about another factor of a successful team—WANTING or MOTIVATION, as the desire is commonly called in the business world!

Out of the many various theories of motivation, I propose focusing on two that work great when applied! :)

MASLOW'S PYRAMID

Maslow's Pyramid is a model that sequentially represents all human needs, from basic to elevated. It reflects one of the most widely recognized motivational concepts — the theory of the hierarchy of needs, developed by psychologist Abraham Maslow. Maslow was a renowned American psychologist, the founder of humanistic psychology, and the creator of the hierarchy of needs model, which is named after him. This model has found broad application in economics due to its clear definition of motivation and consumer behavior.

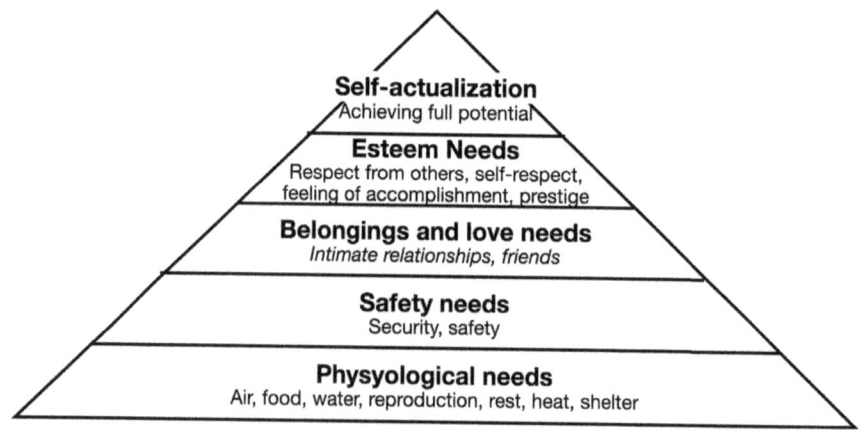

Self-actualization
Achieving full potential

Esteem Needs
Respect from others, self-respect, feeling of accomplishment, prestige

Belongings and love needs
Intimate relationships, friends

Safety needs
Security, safety

Physyological needs
Air, food, water, reproduction, rest, heat, shelter

First, let's break down the pyramid itself and then look at how to interpret this model in an organization. We will start from the bottom and move upwards.

1. The lowest level corresponds to **Physiological Needs** — everything necessary for the survival of our body: air, food, water, sleep, reproduction, etc. A person is capable of doing a lot to satisfy these needs.

For Jesus, the basic needs of people were always important. The Bible contains many examples where Jesus healed diseases, cast out unclean spirits, and provided food for people. This was one of the reasons why people sought Him out and came to Him! After one incident, when Jesus fed thousands of people, the people even wanted to make Him their king!

> *After these things Jesus went over the sea of Galilee, which is the sea of Tiberias. And a great multitude followed him, because they saw his miracles which he did on them that were diseased. And Jesus went up into a mountain, and there he sat with his disciples. And the passover, a feast of the Jews, was nigh. When Jesus then lifted up his eyes, and saw a great company come unto him, he saith unto Philip, Whence shall we buy bread, that these may eat? And this he said to prove him: for he himself knew what he would do. Philip answered him, Two hundred pennyworth of bread is not sufficient for them, that every one of them may take a little. One of his disciples, Andrew, Simon Peter's brother, saith unto him, There is a lad here, which hath five barley loaves, and two small fishes: but what are they among so many? And Jesus said, Make the men sit down. Now there was much grass in the place. So the men sat down, in number about five thousand. And Jesus took the loaves; and when he had given thanks, he distributed to the disciples, and the disciples to them that were set down; and likewise of the fishes as much as they would. When they were filled, he said unto his disciples, Gather up the fragments that remain, that nothing be lost. Therefore they gathered them together, and filled twelve baskets with the fragments of the five barley loaves, which remained over and above unto them that had eaten.*
> *— John 6:1-13*

2. The next level is the level of **Safety**. However, safety here is not in the sense of life-threatening danger — self-preservation instinct is part of the physiological needs level — but in terms of maintaining the existing level of satisfaction of basic needs. This can be generalized as the desire for stability, protection, freedom from fear and anxiety, and the need for order, law, and structure.

The idea that the Lord is our Provider and Protector runs as a red thread throughout the entire Bible! He, Who wisely created each of us, knows all our needs and provides us with everything necessary for life!

> I will praise thee; for I am fearfully and wonderfully made:
> marvellous are thy works; and that my soul knoweth right well.
> — Psalm 139:14

> The LORD is my shepherd; I shall not want. He maketh me to lie
> down in green pastures: he leadeth me beside the still waters. He
> restoreth my soul: he leadeth me in the paths of righteousness for
> his name's sake. Yea, though I walk through the valley of the shadow
> of death, I will fear no evil: for thou art with me; thy rod and thy staff
> they comfort me. Thou preparest a table before me in the presence
> of mine enemies: thou anointest my head with oil; my cup runneth
> over. Surely goodness and mercy shall follow me all the days of my
> life: and I will dwell in the house of the LORD for ever.
> — Psalm 23:1-6

3. The third level is commonly referred to as the level of **Belonging or Love Needs,** which are related to the need for warm, friendly relationships and a social group that will provide such connections. Partially, this need has its roots in human history, where a group of people had much greater chances of survival and development compared to an individual. In practice, this could be family or any other group that accepts and supports a person, where they feel "at home." Certain behaviors, appearance, areas of interest, manners, and social circles are just a few examples of how the third level influences a person's behavior.

Jesus paid special attention to how His followers should behave. Just one of His teachings, the Sermon on the Mount, where He established a new standard of conduct for those who wanted to follow Him, is significant. He often pointed out the difference between what "you have heard" or "was said" and what "I say to you!" Eventually, it was precisely because His followers tried to follow His teachings that they were called "Christians."

Ye have heard that it was said by them of old time, Thou shalt not kill; and whosoever shall kill shall be in danger of the judgment: But I say unto you, That whosoever is angry with his brother without a cause shall be in danger of the judgment: and whosoever shall say to his brother, Raca, shall be in danger of the council: but whosoever shall say, Thou fool, shall be in danger of hell fire.
— Matthew 5:21-22

A new commandment I give unto you, That ye love one another; as I have loved you, that ye also love one another. By this shall all men know that ye are my disciples, if ye have love one to another.
— John 13:34-35

And when he had found him, he brought him unto Antioch. And it came to pass, that a whole year they assembled themselves with the church, and taught much people. And the disciples were called Christians first in Antioch.
— Acts 11:26

This is a true saying, If a man desire the office of a bishop, he desireth a good work. A bishop then must be blameless, the husband of one wife, vigilant, sober, of good behaviour, given to hospitality, apt to teach; Not given to wine, no striker, not greedy of filthy lucre; but patient, not a brawler, not covetous; One that ruleth well his own house, having his children in subjection with all gravity; (For if a man know not how to rule his own house, how shall he take care of the church of God?) Not a novice, lest being lifted up with pride he fall into the condemnation of the devil. Moreover he must have a good report of them which are without; lest he fall into reproach and the snare of the devil. Likewise must the deacons be grave, not double tongued, not given to much wine, not greedy of filthy lucre; Holding the mystery of the faith in a pure conscience. And let these also first be proved; then let them use the office of a deacon, being found blameless. Even so must their wives be grave, not slanderers, sober, faithful in all things. Let the deacons be the husbands of one wife, ruling their children and their own houses

well. For they that have used the office of a deacon well purchase to themselves a good degree, and great boldness in the faith which is in Christ Jesus.
— 1 Timothy 3:1-13

4. The fourth level is associated with **Esteem Needs or Achievement and Recognition**. At this level, what matters to a person is, on one hand, a sense of confidence, independence, and competence, which help them achieve their goals. On the other hand, it involves having respect from others, a certain status, attention, recognition, and possibly even fame.

In many of His parables, Jesus repeatedly drew the attention of His listeners to the fact that those who do the right things will receive a reward and recognition! The listeners understood that by acting in a certain way, they could expect rewards not only in this earthly life but also in eternity!

For the kingdom of heaven is as a man travelling into a far country, who called his own servants, and delivered unto them his goods. And unto one he gave five talents, to another two, and to another one; to every man according to his several ability; and straightway took his journey. Then he that had received the five talents went and traded with the same, and made them other five talents. And likewise he that had received two, he also gained other two. But he that had received one went and digged in the earth, and hid his lord's money. After a long time the lord of those servants cometh, and reckoneth with them. And so he that had received five talents came and brought other five talents, saying, Lord, thou deliveredst unto me five talents: behold, I have gained beside them five talents more. His lord said unto him, Well done, thou good and faithful servant: thou hast been faithful over a few things, I will make thee ruler over many things: enter thou into the joy of thy lord. He also that had received two talents came and said, Lord, thou deliveredst unto me two talents: behold, I have gained two other talents beside them. His lord said unto him, Well done, good and faithful servant; thou hast been faithful over a few things, I will make thee ruler over many things: enter thou into the joy of thy lord. Then he which had received the one talent came and said, Lord, I knew thee that thou art an hard man, reaping where thou hast not sown, and gathering where thou hast not strawed: And I was afraid, and went and hid thy

talent in the earth: lo, there thou hast that is thine. His lord answered and said unto him, Thou wicked and slothful servant, thou knewest that I reap where I sowed not, and gather where I have not strawed: Thou oughtest therefore to have put my money to the exchangers, and then at my coming I should have received mine own with usury. Take therefore the talent from him, and give it unto him which hath ten talents. For unto every one that hath shall be given, and he shall have abundance: but from him that hath not shall be taken away even that which he hath. And cast ye the unprofitable servant into outer darkness: there shall be weeping and gnashing of teeth.
— Matthew 25:14-30

5. Finally, the last level — the level of **Self-Actualization** — is associated with realizing and fulfilling one's calling, life mission, and the ability to achieve it! For every person, it is important to live in harmony and peace with oneself.

Jesus calls us to make decisions in our lives not based on fleeting desires but by focusing on the highest purposes, on our calling, and striving to do the will of the Lord!

Therefore take no thought, saying, What shall we eat? or, What shall we drink? or, Wherewithal shall we be clothed? (For after all these things do the Gentiles seek:) for your heavenly Father knoweth that ye have need of all these things. But seek ye first the kingdom of God, and his righteousness; and all these things shall be added unto you. Take therefore no thought for the morrow: for the morrow shall take thought for the things of itself. Sufficient unto the day is the evil thereof.
— Matthew 6:31-34

Not every one that saith unto me, Lord, Lord, shall enter into the kingdom of heaven; but he that doeth the will of my Father which is in heaven.
— Matthew 7:21

He that loveth father or mother more than me is not worthy of me:
and he that loveth son or daughter more than me is not worthy of
me. And he that taketh not his cross, and followeth after me, is not
worthy of me. He that findeth his life shall lose it: and he that loseth
his life for my sake shall find it.
— Matthew 10:37-39

And whatsoever ye do, do it heartily, as to the Lord, and not unto
men; Knowing that of the Lord ye shall receive the reward of the
inheritance: for ye serve the Lord Christ.
— Colossians 3:23-24

Before moving forward, I suggest answering a few questions:

1. Can a person be motivated by several needs simultaneously, or does everything develop progressively?

The fact that you are hungry or feel some other physiological need does not mean that you disregard all other needs! For example, if you're hungry, you wouldn't immediately resort to theft or violence to satisfy that hunger, would you? Moreover, if you're offered to do something that contradicts your values or moral beliefs in exchange for food, you would probably refuse or hesitate for a long time. Every person experiences the full spectrum of needs at any given moment. However, at any particular time, there are dominant needs — something that is more important compared to others and that ultimately drives a person to action. Based on this, the person makes decisions!

2. Why a pyramid, and not another shape, like a circle or a square?

Originally, Maslow did not suggest it in this shape. It appeared later. Partly, the arrangement of the levels and their size corresponds to the number of people who are motivated by different needs. The majority of people make decisions primarily based on their physiological needs. The higher up you go, the fewer people are driven by the motivators of the higher levels. Does this mean that these needs are less important or weaker? Not at all! The higher the motivator, the stronger and more lasting it is! Hunger makes itself known every 6-12 hours, while the feeling of victory or achieving something you were part of can inspire you for months or even years.

This explains why the pyramid model is used — because it reflects how human motivations evolve and the relative strength and sustainability of those motivations at different levels.

3. Can one be motivated by higher levels while lower levels are not fully satisfied?

At first glance, this seems unlikely. To think about safety, one must first have something! Only when there's some status and provision can one think about family and social belonging. Respect and authority are certainly important, just as is self-realization, but that comes later; right now, the need is to satisfy immediate desires at any cost, right?

However, let's look at the example of our Lord Jesus Christ. Was recognition and a struggle for authority among the ruling class of His time important to Him? No! He wasn't seeking to please the Pharisees and the rulers of that time! His speech, where He said "woe to you" seven times, illustrates this perfectly!

Was social status important to Him? No! He avoided communities that wanted to proclaim Him king, and sometimes He consciously confronted wealthy people! On the contrary, He was often seen in the company of tax collectors and sinners.

Was safety important to Him? No! Even though they tried to stone Him several times in Judea, He returned there! When instructing His disciples, He told them not to take money with them and not to worry about provision!

Were physiological needs important to Him? No! Jesus could certainly have had better food, but He was content with bread and fish, just like the thousands of people around Him! Moreover, He often spent nights in prayer, didn't have a wife…

So, what was important to Him? What motivated Him? The awareness of His atoning mission and His desire to fulfill the will of the Father came above all, and ultimately, it led Jesus to the cross, where He voluntarily gave His life for many!

This shows that even when lower levels of needs are not fully satisfied, higher motivations — rooted in purpose, mission, or calling — can drive action and decisions.

Let's now look at the practical application of Maslow's Pyramid in an organization:

1. **Physiological Needs:** These are addressed by salaries, bonuses, commissions, benefits (such as discounts on food, products, or services, transportation allowances, etc.).

2. **Safety Needs:** These are covered by the employment contract, work schedule, administrative regulations, and disciplinary measures.

3. **Belongingness Needs:** These are supported by company traditions, shared events, uniforms or style and appearance guidelines, certain behavior and etiquette rules.

4. **Esteem Needs:** These are fulfilled through public praise, awards or trophies, assigning new tasks, opportunities for training, and career advancement.

5. **Self-Actualization Needs:** These are achieved by discussing individual development plans, through the example set by the leader, and building relationships with senior colleagues or those in higher positions within the organization.

By addressing each level of needs, organizations can create a motivated, engaged, and productive workforce, which is essential for long-term success and growth.

Reflective task:

Conduct a review of the motivators in your organization and, for each level of Maslow's pyramid, create a list of what you currently have. Suggest ideas for each level that could complement this list.

HERZBERG MODEL

Frederick Irving Herzberg was an American psychologist who developed the principles of the two-factor motivation theory and introduced the concepts of hygiene factors and motivating factors, or, in other words, the working conditions and the content of the work itself.

In conducting research at several large companies, he asked employees to describe situations where their work brought them particular satisfaction and when they especially disliked it. As a result of the research, Herzberg concluded that job satisfaction and dissatisfaction are determined by two different groups of factors, which can be described as factors that keep people on the job and factors that motivate them to work.

Factors that cause job dissatisfaction — known as **Hygiene factors** or **Hygiene** — are related to the working conditions or environment where the work is performed. These include company policies, working conditions, salary levels, and interpersonal relationships with supervisors, colleagues, and subordinates. A lack of or deficiency in hygiene factors leads to dissatisfaction with work. However, even if they are adequately provided, they do not, by themselves, generate satisfaction or motivate an employee to take necessary action. In such cases, an employee simply "goes to work" and puts in the minimum effort required to complete the tasks.

Factors that cause job satisfaction — known as **Motivating factors** or **Motivators** — are related to the content of the work itself, its nature, and its essence. These include achievement, recognition of accomplishments, responsibility, and opportunities for career growth. The absence of motivating factors does not necessarily cause dissatisfaction with work. However, their presence creates satisfaction and motivates employees to take action, increasing work efficiency and productivity.

Motivators and Hygiene Factors	Negative Influence	Positive Influence
Achivement		
Recognition		
Interest in work		
Responsibility		
Career growth		
Professional growth		
Management style		
Administrative policies		
Interpersonal relationships/ boss		
Working conditions		
Renumeration		
Interpersonal relationships/ colleagues		
Work-lifetime balance		
Interpersonal relationships/subordinates		
Uncertainty		

The graph shows a list of **hygiene** and **motivating** factors. The position of the factors on the **vertical axis** can be interpreted as the **strength of influence**. In other words, the higher the factor, the stronger its impact on employee behavior.

The **horizontal length** of a factor's line can be interpreted as the **duration of its influence**, which reflects how frequently a particular factor was mentioned during research. If a certain factor is insufficiently present or appears in a negative context, any of these factors can act as a **demotivator.**

For example, most of us enjoy setting and achieving goals. However, if goals are not achieved for some reason, this can lead to disappointment and insecurity. A salary increase is generally perceived positively and influences employee behavior for about **two to three months**. However, during this period, an employee's expenses typically adjust to the new income level, and they begin to see the increased salary as standard. Afterward, the employee may once again feel "**undervalued**," which could lead to job dissatisfaction.

Let's take a closer look at each of these factors.

HYGIENE FACTORS:

Management Style: The level and style of control from management that affects the working atmosphere. Example: Degree of employee autonomy, presence of micromanagement, or trust from management in employees' ability to perform their duties.

Administrative policies (Supervision and Oversight): The policies and procedures that regulate work within the company. Example: Transparent and fair rules and procedures, vacation and working hour policies.

Interpersonal Relationships with the Boss, Colleagues and Subordinates**:** The quality of interaction with colleagues, supervisors, and subordinates. Example: A friendly and supportive atmosphere, respectful relationships with management.

Working Conditions: The quality, comfort, and safety of the workspace; availability of necessary resources. Example: Clean and comfortable office, ergonomic furniture, availability of necessary tools and equipment.

Renumeration (Salary and Additional Benefits): The level of compensation, including salary, bonuses, and financial benefits. Example: Fair and competitive salary, bonuses, and insurance payments.

Job Security and Stability: Confidence in long-term employment and protection from arbitrary dismissal. Example: Job security, absence of termination threats.

MOTIVATORS:

Achievement: A sense of pride in accomplished successes and completed tasks. Example: Completion of major projects, achieving set goals.

Recognition and Respect: Acknowledgment of employee achievements and contributions to the team or company's success. Example: Recognition of success, awards for achievements.

Interest in Work: Enjoyment of the work itself and a sense of its significance. Example: Working on interesting and meaningful projects, with creative freedom in problem-solving.

Responsibility: The ability to make important decisions and be accountable for results. Example: Independence in work, freedom to make decisions.

Promotion: Recognition in the form of moving to higher positions. Example: Promotion within the company, career growth.

Personal/Professional Development: Opportunities for professional and personal growth, learning, and self-improvement. Example: Participation in training and seminars, as well as career advancement.

According to Herzberg's model, there are four possible combinations of hygiene and motivating factors:

Low Hygiene + High Motivation	High Hygiene + High Motivation
Here, employees are motivated by the work itself but are dissatisfied with the working conditions. This often leads to frustration despite the desire to perform well. Example: Exciting and meaningful projects but poor working conditions or unfair policies.	This is the ideal situation where employees are highly motivated, and the working environment is supportive. Employees are satisfied with their work and inspired to perform at a high level. Example: Fair compensation, strong team spirit, and opportunities for professional growth.
Low Hygiene + Low Motivation	**High Hygiene + Low Motivation**
This is the worst-case scenario where employees are neither satisfied with their work environment nor motivated to perform well. This leads to high turnover and low productivity. Example: Low pay, poor working conditions, lack of recognition, and no career growth opportunities.	In this case, employees are not dissatisfied with the working environment, but they are not motivated to go above and beyond. Work is seen as stable but unfulfilling. Example: Competitive salary and good working conditions, but lack of recognition or career growth opportunities.

Hygiene factors help to remove dissatisfaction and ensure that employees are not unhappy with their working conditions. However, they don't necessarily motivate employees to go above and beyond. On the other hand, motivating factors are what truly inspire employees to be more engaged, productive, and fulfilled in their roles.

When both hygiene and motivating factors are in harmony, it creates a balanced and positive work environment that fosters both satisfaction and motivation. Employees are not only content with the conditions they work in but also feel inspired to contribute more, innovate, and grow within the organization.

A well-balanced mix of both is key to ensuring long-term success and employee retention in any workplace.

FOOD FOR THOUGHT:

Often, organizational or department managers complain that low results are the consequence of low salary levels. Is that the case?

Salaries on your project should be competitive. What does "competitive" mean? You can use publicly available information about the average salary level for specific positions, which can be found on the websites of companies that offer recruitment services.

In this regard, let's look at factors that go beyond salaries, and therefore have a higher potential for impact. Evaluate the costs associated with utilizing them. You've probably noticed that often, these costs are close to "zero"!

How much does it cost to give attention and formulate SMART goals for an employee (SMART stands for Specific, Measurable, Achievable, Realistic, Time-bound)? It's just the manager's time to dive into the task, assess the employee's level of competence, and agree on the task with them! But this could result in feeling success and achievement.

How much does recognition cost? The manager just needs to acknowledge the level of task completion and praise the employee, preferably publicly.

What are the costs of forming a correct understanding of the nature of the job and responsibility? It's important for the manager to properly organize the onboarding of a new employee, adapt their management style to the employee's level of competence, avoid micromanagement, and refrain from excessive control. When communicating with the employee, it's crucial to emphasize the importance of their role and contribution to the shared goal! How much does this cost the company?

However, often, even with a competitive salary level, you still cannot achieve higher work efficiency and productivity. This is usually because the manager underestimates the role of motivating factors and, instead of focusing on motivating factors, prefers to take the path of least resistance (for themselves) by adjusting salaries.

Reflective task:

Conduct a review of the hygiene factors and motivators in your organization. Propose actions or measures for each factor that could strengthen it.

The Second Leg of the Tabouret Principle: the Team — Executing

Executing — to carry (something) out fully; to put (something) completely into effect; to do what is provided or required by (something).

If you can confidently answer "yes" to the statements below, it means that this component of successful work is, to some extent, implemented in your project:

- You have implemented The First Leg of the Tabouret Principle (System)

- The results of each team member have objective evaluation criteria, and their monitoring takes place regularly (weekly, monthly, quarterly, yearly) with subsequent discussion of the outcomes, setting new tasks, and agreeing on an action plan to achieve them

Therefore whosoever heareth these sayings of mine, and doeth them, I will liken him unto a wise man, which built his house upon a rock: And the rain descended, and the floods came, and the winds blew, and beat upon that house; and it fell not: for it was founded upon a rock. And every one that heareth these sayings of mine, and doeth them not, shall be likened unto a foolish man, which built his house upon the sand: And the rain descended, and the floods came, and the winds blew, and beat upon that house; and it fell: and great was the fall of it.
— *Matthew 7:24-27*

Jesus emphasized the importance of putting His words into practice! According to the parable mentioned above, becoming a disciple of Jesus does not guarantee a trouble-free life. However, if a person not only listens but also follows the commandments of Jesus, then even when serious trials come, they will be able to withstand them and stand firm through difficulties.

We don't know for sure the exact reasons why Eve and later Adam chose to break the Creator's command and eat the forbidden fruit. They knew it was forbidden. They had plenty of alternative options that could meet their needs (Knowing and Being Able). It's unlikely that their goal was to offend or grieve God (Wanting). Nevertheless, what happened, and they did what they did!

As a result, feelings of shame and fear arose, leading them to hide from God. Later, in their children — Cain and Abel— these feelings transformed into envy, violence, and deception. And only because Jesus took the punishment for the sins of the whole world, each of us can now receive the unconditional love and forgiveness of our Heavenly Father!

Every organization where team members know what to do and how to do it, have the necessary skills and can effectively apply them to solve various tasks, desire to achieve goals and succeed, and most importantly, EXECUTE the necessary actions — will be successful!

EXECUTING is the final link in this chain, without which everything else has little meaning! Responsibility partially rests on the leader as long as an employee lacks knowledge, skills, or motivation. Of course, the employee is also expected to put in effort and show initiative to master the necessary knowledge and skills as quickly as possible.

However, once the employee has received the necessary support and resources from the company and the leader, it becomes their responsibility to put in the effort and achieve the goals! In this sense, EXECUTING is 100% the employee's responsibility!

If you've carefully studied the materials from the First leg of The Tabouret Principle and completed the tasks, it shouldn't be difficult for you to determine whether an employee is doing what's required or not! Every task has clear criteria. Thanks to the monitoring system, you can always see the outcome.

If there are results or fruits — that means it's being executed. If there are no results or fruits — that means it's not being executed.

It's important to keep in mind that we work in a team. If someone is showing poor results and the leadership turns a blind eye to it, this sends the wrong signal to the rest of the team: "Nothing bad will happen if you perform poorly." Over time, this can lead to serious losses.

Unfortunately, I've sometimes encountered situations where believing leaders didn't quite understand their role as leaders. One of my partners, during a discussion about dismissing a team member, once remarked that Jesus never fired anyone — even Judas, who betrayed Him and whom He knew would betray Him, was not cast out!

As part of the **"DreamTeam"** team management training, which is also built on biblical principles, we explore the **"Team Management Cycle"** based on the model of "Knowing, Being Able, Wanting, and Executing."

If a leader faces unsatisfactory results, their primary task is to figure out the root cause!

If the issue is due to gaps in "Knowing" — the leader should arrange measures to fill the knowledge gaps.

If the problem is with skills — that is, "Being Able" — the gap in skills should be addressed.

If the challenge lies in motivation — "Wanting" — the leader needs to solve this issue.

But if the employee knows, can, wants, and still doesn't perform — meaning there are still no results — then there's only one solution left.

How did the Lord respond when humanity broke His commandment? The Lord "sent" or "drove" humanity out of the Garden of Eden. In our case, this refers to termination.

Of course, it would be too hasty to immediately part ways with an employee at the first sign of trouble. However, if these "issues" arise regularly, then a decision needs to be made. Each manager sets their own boundaries depending on their management style, external conditions, and the importance of the task...

In my case, I followed approximately this approach: First of all, I tried to make sure that my employee knew, was able, and wanted.

How did this look in practice? When summarizing the results of a reporting period and encountering unsatisfactory results, I would meet individually with the relevant employee. During the conversation, by asking questions, I would try to identify areas of concern.

If it worked out, we would agree on an action plan to fill the gaps and set new goals.

If, after the conversation, I concluded that the employee had the necessary knowledge and skills, was motivated, but for some other reason the result was below the agreed goal, then for the first time, I would limit myself to pointing out the inadmissibility of such results and emphasize the importance of each team member taking responsibility for achieving goals! I did not resort to any administrative penalties, such as a reprimand.

This could happen several times. If the situation didn't improve, I would start looking for a replacement and prepare for dismissal.

FOOD FOR THOUGHT:

While working at one of the international companies as a sales manager, I faced a situation where one of my team members, who was working in another city, had been showing unsatisfactory results for several reporting periods.

I traveled to meet him, and we spent an entire day together, having many meetings with both retail and wholesale clients.

By the end of the day, I identified what needed to be changed and agreed on an action plan with the employee.

Before I left, the employee shared with me: "Thank you for coming. It feels like my eyes have been opened! Great! Everything will be different now!"

A few months later, I visited him again because his results were still disappointing. Once again, we spent the whole day together.

By the end of the day, I could see that he had sufficient knowledge and skills and, according to him, was motivated enough. We reviewed the day, discussed the action plan — and at the end of our meeting, I heard almost the exact same phrase he had said the last time…

A month later, a new employee was hired in that city.

I would like to draw your attention to the fact that termination should not be seen as a tragedy —either for yourself or for the employee.

I can recall many situations where people who struggled to perform well in one position later adapted and achieved remarkable success elsewhere.

One of the most striking cases is related to my work in the massage equipment sales business. Since it was based on a franchise model, each franchisee hired their own employees, who were indirectly accountable to the main company.

One of the employees in this business showed very weak results. After discussing the situation, we concluded that he had the knowledge and skills and claimed to be motivated — but… he simply wasn't taking action.

As a result, we decided to part ways.

Sometime later, I learned that this person had become a highly successful DJ (MC)!

Just imagine — if we had continued working together, where neither he nor we were satisfied with the results, he might never have fulfilled his true calling!

Reflective task:

Taking into account the information regarding your team, conduct a review of the system within your organization.

Propose specific actions or measures that will allow you to clearly see the results or outcomes of each specific task.

The Second Leg of the Tabouret Principle: the Partners — Benefit Today

Benefit — something that produces good or helpful results or effects or that promotes well-being.

If you can confidently answer "yes" to the statements below, it means that this component of successful work is, to some extent, implemented in your project:

- You have information about the cost of goods/services and the terms of cooperation for each direction in which you engage counterparties

- You regularly monitor the market for similar counterparties to identify changes in prices or terms of collaboration

- Based on this monitoring, you hold meetings to discuss and agree on prices for goods/services and/or terms of mutually beneficial cooperation.

Then said the LORD unto Moses, Behold, I will rain bread from heaven for you; and the people shall go out and gather a certain rate every day, that I may prove them, whether they will walk in my law, or no. And it shall come to pass, that on the sixth day they shall prepare that which they bring in; and it shall be twice as much as they gather daily.
— Exodus 16:4-5

Therefore I say unto you, Take no thought for your life, what ye shall eat, or what ye shall drink; nor yet for your body, what ye shall put on. Is not the life more than meat, and the body than raiment? Behold the fowls of the air: for they sow not, neither do they reap, nor gather into barns; yet your heavenly Father feedeth them. Are ye not much better than they? Which of you by taking thought can add one cubit unto his stature? And why take ye thought for raiment? Consider the lilies of the field, how they grow; they toil not, neither do they spin: And yet I say unto you, That even Solomon in all his glory was not arrayed like one of these. Wherefore, if God so clothe the grass of the field, which to day is, and to morrow is cast into the oven, shall he not much more clothe you, O ye of little faith? Therefore take no thought, saying, What shall we eat? or, What shall we drink? or, Wherewithal shall we be clothed? (For after all these things do the Gentiles seek:) for your heavenly Father knoweth that ye have need of all these things. But seek ye first the kingdom of God, and his righteousness; and all these things shall be added unto you.
— Matthew 6:25-33

The Bible is filled with many examples of God's love and care! We don't often think about it, but every moment, billions of processes are occurring in our bodies that keep us alive and give us the ability to live! We usually only realize this when we feel limitations or fall ill. Scientists have concluded that the balance of gases in the air is unique! If the balance were disrupted, we wouldn't be able to breathe! The sun gives light and warmth, water, and earth—we are surrounded by God's care and grace! If the sun was any closer, it would burn our planet; if it were further, the planet would freeze. This and many other examples around us are manifestations of our Creator's partnership with each of us! You'll agree, if you have partners like this, it will be much easier to develop your project.

· Alex Marchuk ·

No matter what your project's goal is — whether it's to make a profit or a non-profit activity — you will generally need partners or a contractor.

Contractor (from Late Latin contractor "party to a contract," from Latin contrac-, variant stem of contrahere "to draw together, reduce in size, bring together, enter into (an agreement, formal relationship) — one that contracts or is party to a contract; one that contracts to perform work or provide supplies.

A contractor is any organization you interact with. Do you have a bank account? Your bank is your contractor. Do you rent an office or a warehouse? Do you use mobile services or the internet? Do you rely on delivery services or run advertisements? Every company that provides you with goods or services is a contractor.

The English have a saying: "A fleet is only as fast as its slowest ship!" Think about it — even if you have the fastest boats, they still need fuel and maintenance. If the support services are lagging, the frontline fleet won't be able to operate efficiently either. For the fleet to be quick and effective, all its components — including supply and support — need to function at top speed.

The same applies to projects. If you have contractors, you need to find and build relationships with those who can strengthen you and contribute to meeting the needs of your target audience in the best possible way! Otherwise, you'll waste time and resources trying to make up for the shortcomings of your contractors.

To select a contractor that offers the most attractive terms, you need to analyze market offers, review websites and feedback, hold meetings with representatives of potential contractors, and choose those who, on one hand, provide the best conditions right now, and on the other — have the potential to build long-term relationships.

FOOD FOR THOUGHT

This story is about cycling and highlights the importance of small, seemingly insignificant details (we've already mentioned Kaizen earlier).

Before the early 2000s, British cycling was far from being at the top of the world stage. In 2003, the British Cycling Federation appointed Sir Dave Brailsford as the head of the cycling program at British Cycling. One of the key innovations introduced by Sir Brailsford was the Principle of Marginal Gains. The idea behind this principle is to aim for small improvements

— just a few percentage points — in every detail or process, with the belief that the combined effect of these small gains will lead to significant overall results.

Dave Brailsford and his team began analyzing and optimizing literally every aspect of training and competition. Here are some examples of how they applied this principle:

Aerodynamics: They measured the aerodynamic characteristics of the bikes and gear, which led to improvements in the design and materials of bike frames, wheels, helmets, and uniforms.

Nutrition and Training: After analyzing the athletes' diets, nutritionists created tailored meal plans to maximize performance. Individualized training programs were also introduced for each athlete.

Rest: The team focused on sleep quality by providing specially designed pillows and mattresses, ensuring better recovery at team hotels. They also adjusted the lighting and temperature in training and competition environments.

Recovery: Specialized hygiene protocols were introduced to prevent and control the spread of colds and infections. Targeted massage procedures were also implemented to speed up muscle recovery.

Psychological Preparation: Personalized mental training programs were introduced to enhance stress resilience and improve focus. Individual goal-setting and motivation plans were also created.

The results didn't take long to show. In 2008, Great Britain dominated the Beijing Olympics, winning 8 gold medals in cycling. At the 2012 London Olympics, British cyclists once again came out on top, securing another 8 gold medals. In 2012, Briton Bradley Wiggins won the Tour de France, becoming the first British rider to achieve this victory. His success was repeated by Chris Froome, who won the Tour de France in 2013, 2015, 2016, and 2017.

The story of Team Sky and their success in applying the Principle of Marginal Gains shows how small improvements across different areas can combine to produce outstanding achievements and victories. By applying this approach to both your internal processes and your contractors, you can achieve remarkable results in your project.

Sometimes, when comparing proposals from potential contractors and noticing minor differences (such as bank payment processing fees, mobile or internet service rates, office or warehouse rent, etc.), you might wonder whether it's even worth making changes to improve them. Maybe it's not.

In any case, I recommend evaluating not just abstract percentages or rates, but also estimating your potential expenses over a month, a quarter, or a year. Sometimes figures that seem minor in absolute terms can translate into significant savings over the course of a month or a year!

The same applies to working conditions. If you can secure trade credit or pay for services a week or a month after receiving them — or if goods are delivered to you for free instead of you covering the shipping costs — this can significantly reduce the strain on your working capital and enable more dynamic growth.

The benefits that your project can gain today are a crucial factor in deciding on the development and establishment of long-term partnerships with a particular contractor.

Reflective task:

Based on the information received, review the terms offered by your current contractors. To do this, analyze similar offers available on the market for each contractor.

Create a comparison table that evaluates the attractiveness of your existing contractor's terms against alternative options. Include key criteria such as:

· Cost of services/products

· Payment terms

· Delivery terms

· Quality of service/product

· Additional benefits (e.g., trade credit, free shipping)

Hold meetings with potential contractors to assess their potential for building long-term relationships. Consider factors like:

· Flexibility in adjusting terms

· Willingness to collaborate

· Communication and responsiveness

Their track record and market reputation

Evaluate the findings to determine whether switching to a new contractor could provide better overall value or if renegotiating terms with the current contractor is a more strategic move.

The Second Leg of the Tabouret: the Partners — Stability

Stability (from Latin stabilis, from stare to stand) — the quality, state, or degree of being stable: firmly established; not changing or fluctuating; steady in purpose.

If you can confidently answer "yes" to the statements below, it means that this component of successful work is, to some extent, implemented in your project:

- You have implemented the "The First Leg of the Tabouret Principle: System"

- The performance of each contractor is measured using objective indicators that are monitored regularly (weekly, monthly, quarterly, annually).

- The monitoring results are discussed consistently, followed by setting new tasks and agreeing on action plans to improve outcomes.

And Noah builded an altar unto the LORD; and took of every clean beast, and of every clean fowl, and offered burnt offerings on the altar. And the LORD smelled a sweet savour; and the LORD said in his heart, I will not again curse the ground any more for man's sake; for the imagination of man's heart is evil from his youth; neither will I again smite any more every thing living, as I have done. While the earth remaineth, seedtime and harvest, and cold and heat, and summer and winter, and day and night shall not cease.
— Genesis 8:20-23

For I am persuaded, that neither death, nor life, nor angels, nor principalities, nor powers, nor things present, nor things to come, Nor height, nor depth, nor any other creature, shall be able to separate us from the love of God, which is in Christ Jesus our Lord.
— Romans 8:38-39

After the flood, Noah could have essentially made himself a god — no one would have stopped him. Yet instead, Noah built an altar and honored the true God! Noah's faithfulness led to the Lord making a covenant about the future of the earth.

Our Great and Good Heavenly Father remains faithful to His promises, no matter our failings! Abraham fathered a son with his servant, even though the Lord had clearly told him that He would bless his descendants through Sarah. Abraham also lied more than once about Sarah being his sister. Yet despite this, the Lord continued to support and bless him.

Our God is unchanging. He is faithful to His promises. Stability is another key characteristic of partnership, which is crucial for building long-term relationships.

FOOD FOR THOUGHT:

After repentance, when I learned that our names are written in the Book of Life, I initially lived with the feeling that every time I did something good, my name was like being written again, and when I made mistakes, my name was wiped away like with an eraser. This led to disappointment, unnecessary stress, and anxiety, especially with myself! On the other hand, when I felt I hadn't sinned, I felt some condemnation filling my heart towards those who did something wrong. Even more so, I expected some special reward for my "righteous" actions, and when I didn't receive what I expected, I felt something like resentment towards the Heavenly Father. "How is this? I'm so good, but the circumstances around me don't seem to favor me!"

Over time, I came to realize that righteousness and forgiveness are gifts from God, not dependent on my actions but on my ability to believe and receive them! God's righteousness is not a ceiling, not something I can attain with all my might! It is the foundation, the starting point for my life, building relationships, and making decisions! Our Heavenly Father is Holy, Good, and Merciful! Like the father in the parable of the prodigal son, He always expects that we will come to Him, to open His arms, and call each of us His child! And the feeling of this, the certainty of who our God is, along with forgiveness and righteousness, gives strength, confidence, hope, joy, and peace!

For any project, **Stability** is crucial. If you have contractors, you plan your actions based on the prices, terms, and agreements that have been reached. Of course, you are interested in ensuring that these terms and agreements are upheld! Any change in conditions from your contractor or a breakdown in operations typically leads to your losses! Therefore, one of the key parameters that determines the value and potential for long-term cooperation is Stability!

FOOD FOR THOUGHT:

In the context of a "Negotiation Skills" seminar, we analyze key negotiation markers: "Opening," "Optimal Outcome," and "Exit Point." Each position corresponds to a set of conditions and concessions from both sides, which ultimately affect the negotiation result.

The "Opening" typically represents the minimum level of concessions on your part and the maximum level of demands from the counterparty. The "Optimal Outcome" assumes a balance of concessions from both sides. The "Exit Point" refers to a list of the counterparty's demands that are unacceptable to you, and if they insist on them, it signals that you must walk away from the negotiation.

The list and scope of conditions and concessions for each negotiation position should be determined in advance, with adjustments made as the negotiation process develops. This helps you protect yourself from various manipulative negotiation techniques while also allowing you to assert your position clearly and with strong reasoning.

· Alex Marchuk ·

When discussing the terms of cooperation with any partner, you need to have a clear understanding of what has been agreed upon and how it impacts your project. In the event of changes in prices or cooperation terms, it is important to assess how these new parameters will affect the outcomes of your project. You should always focus on what will make your project stronger.

If you have a clear representation of the parameters you expect as a result of existing prices and terms for each partner, you can regularly monitor them and, in the end, provide feedback to your partners. Just as a restaurant owner values the guest's opinion about the food and service, the managers and owners of your partners value the feedback from their customers! This feedback helps your partners improve and enables the development of long-term, trust-based relationships.

FOOD FOR THOUGHT:

In the context of a "Negotiation Skills" seminar, we also examine negotiation tactics and ways to protect ourselves from manipulative actions by the other party. One such manipulation is called "Salami." The idea is that salami is traditionally eaten in very thin slices. If I asked you for half a stick of salami, you would likely refuse. But if I ask for just one or a few very thin slices, it would seem harmless, and you might think it's okay to give a couple of slices. The problem is, this request will be followed by another, and another, and soon you'll realize, to your surprise, that you've given away the same half-stick of salami!

This tactic is sometimes used in negotiations and involves being asked for a small concession, while at the same time being told that this small concession will lead to a big benefit. How should you react? If you have prepared your negotiation positions in advance, you will be able to properly assess the size of the concession and the potential benefit—knowing your "exit point" helps. If you're being pushed to go beyond that point, you will know what to do. In any case, if you're unsure about something or receive new information that requires careful consideration, it's always a good practice to take a pause and reassess all the "pros" and "cons." It's normal for negotiations to be paused for consultation. Making a decision without this could be reckless and lead to losses!

Reflective task:

Based on the information received, evaluate the parameters that describe the collaboration with each contractor. Regularly monitor these parameters and track their alignment with your agreements and market conditions.

Hold regular meetings with your contractors and provide them with feedback on your collaboration.

The Second Leg of the Tabouret: the Partners — Perspective

Perspective (from Latin prospectus view, prospect, from prospicere to look forward, exercise foresight) — a mental view or prospect; the interrelation in which a subject or its parts are mentally viewed; the capacity to view things in their true relations or relative importance.

If you can confidently answer "yes" to the statements below, it means that this component of successful work is, to some extent, implemented in your project:

- You have implemented **"The First Leg of the Tabouret Principle: System"**

- You are familiar with key employees, the management, and possibly the owners of the organizations that are your partners. You are aware of their competitive advantages, their vision, values, and strategies, just as they are familiar with this information about your organization.

And he brought him forth abroad, and said, Look now toward heaven, and tell the stars, if thou be able to number them: and he said unto him, So shall thy seed be. And he believed in the LORD; and he counted it to him for righteousness.
— Genesis 15:5-6

And I will give unto thee, and to thy seed after thee, the land wherein thou art a stranger, all the land of Canaan, for an everlasting possession; and I will be their God.
— Genesis 17:8

For I know the thoughts that I think toward you, saith the LORD, thoughts of peace, and not of evil, to give you an expected end.
— Jeremiah 29:11

And I saw a new heaven and a new earth: for the first heaven and the first earth were passed away; and there was no more sea. And I John saw the holy city, new Jerusalem, coming down from God out of heaven, prepared as a bride adorned for her husband. And I heard a great voice out of heaven saying, Behold, the tabernacle of God is with men, and he will dwell with them, and they shall be his people, and God himself shall be with them, and be their God. And God shall wipe away all tears from their eyes; and there shall be no more death, neither sorrow, nor crying, neither shall there be any more pain: for the former things are passed away.
— Revelation 21:1-4

The Lord, as a Partner, inspired and supported Abraham's faith by giving him perspective. The stars, the sand — these are real, visible images that helped Abraham understand how numerous his descendants would be! For each of us believers, it's not only about the forgiveness of sins here and now, but also about the promises related to eternal life with our Almighty Great Creator!

Why is perspective so important? For several reasons.

First, by having perspective, you can better understand what and how you need to do things to approach it with greater readiness! Understanding the perspective will give you the ability to set priorities and be more conscious and rational in making decisions: if a decision brings you closer to the perspective, it's worth pursuing; if not, it's worth considering other alternatives!

Secondly, when things are tough, and it seems like circumstances are against you, you can miraculously receive encouragement and reinforcement because you have a vision of, as I call it, the best future in Christ"!

Why is perspective important in partnership? If your partners are growing and implementing newer, more efficient, and productive technologies, your offering usually improves as well! If the delivery service can bring the order in 1-2 days instead of 3-5 days, you win! If the bank can process a payment online without the accountant having to visit the branch, you win! If you can accept payments online from clients, you win! And so on…

Imagine that your partner is not evolving. They have a business model that works today and brings in revenue. What will happen tomorrow if technologies advance? What if your partner becomes disillusioned with this direction and decides to pivot to something else? It will take time for you to find a new partner in their place. Furthermore, don't forget that with new partners, you will need to build relationships and earn trust, which will take your time and other resources that could have been directed elsewhere.

Reflective task:

Taking into account the received information:

a. *Assess how well you know the key employees, managers, and possibly the owners of the companies that are your partners;*

b. *Assess how well you understand their competitive advantages, vision, values, strategies, and whether they know the same information about your organization;*

c. *Plan and conduct meetings dedicated to discussing the future of your cooperation;*

d. *Agree to and hold similar meetings on a regular basis.*

Key conclusions of the section The Second Leg of the Tabouret: the Team and the Partners

The Second Leg of the Tabouret Principle Represents the Team and the Partners.

For a Team to function effectively, each member must:

1. **Know** – this refers to having information about the organization, its products or services, standards, and systems necessary to perform tasks.

2. **Be Able** – this relates to developing a specific set of skills and competencies required to complete tasks.

3. **Be Wanting** – this involves using various tools to motivate and engage employees.

4. **Execute** – this refers to monitoring and ensuring the quality and completion of assigned tasks.

For a Partnership to be effective, the following principles must be upheld:

1. **Benefit Today** – this means having competitive terms of cooperation.

2. **Stability** – this refers to maintaining consistent and reliable conditions for collaboration.

3. **Perspective** – this relates to the strategy and development plans of the organizations involved.

Reflective task:

Review the materials of the section "The Second Leg of the Tabouret Principle: the Team and the Partners."

Highlight (underline, mark with a highlighter, make notes in the margins, etc.) the areas that you think should be shared with your team.
Plan where and how you can do this.

Based on your understanding of the current state of the project, assess the presence of the "Second Leg of the Tabouret Principle" in each department. Invite the responsible employees and agree on goals together, then create an implementation plan.

The Third Leg of the Tabouret Principle: the Followers

And God blessed them, and God said unto them, Be fruitful, and
multiply, and replenish the earth, and subdue it: and have dominion
over the fish of the sea, and over the fowl of the air, and over every
living thing that moveth upon the earth.
— Genesis 1:28

When speaking about "be fruitful and multiply," I am sure that the Lord did not mean exclusively the physiological process of reproduction. Otherwise, when Cain killed Abel, the Lord could have responded something like: "It's not a big deal, you can have more children!" This is about succession, about passing on personal relationships between God and His creation! It's about those who will know God, honor His commandments, and relate to Him. And this is our third leg — FOLLOWERS.

Follower — one in the service of another; one that follows the opinions or teachings of another; one that imitates another.

Followers play a key role in the longevity of a project. If there are many of them and their number is growing, the project will have steady development. If there are few or their number is decreasing, the project is likely to be closed in the future. In the Gospels of Matthew and Luke, one can find the genealogy of Jesus Christ from Adam is presented! How wonderful it is that despite all circumstances, the succession was preserved, and eventually, the Savior for the whole world appeared! Even in the darkest times, when the prophet Elijah, crying out to the Lord, said that he alone remained faithful to Him, in response, he heard:

Yet I have left me seven thousand in Israel, all the knees which have not bowed unto Baal, and every mouth which hath not kissed him.
— 1 Kings 19:18

When we talk about followers, we're not only referring to clients or recipients. Not at all. Followers can be both your clients and your employees or partners. If, instead of indifferent and passive team members or careless partners, you have passionate and dedicated followers, there's a great chance that your organization will thrive! Let's look at the potential consequences of this in everyday activities:

	Criteria	**Actions that destroy**	**Actions that build up**
Team	Attitude to the job	Works 'just okay' Does not show initiative	Works with enthusiasm Shows initiative Sets an example
	Attitude to the Partners or Contractors	Neglect or dismissive attitude	Respectful attitude, as we have a common cause Help and support
	Attitude to the Clients or Addressees	Lack of interest in the customer	Show genuine interest Develop relationships
Partners/ Contractors	Attitude toward fulfilling agreements	Violation of agreements or terms	Fulfill agreements
	Attitude toward other project participants	Neglect or dismissive attitude	Respectful attitude Coordination of actions
Clients/ Addresses	Attitude to the organization or product/service	Lack of loyalty	High loyalty
	Attitude toward other clients or recipients	Neglect or dismissive attitude	Active involvement in the project

Every person who interacts with your project in one way or another can become its follower! Of course, you'd want that to happen. However, first of all, it doesn't happen on its own. And secondly, even if you take the right actions, it doesn't guarantee a 100% result!

And he spake many things unto them in parables, saying, Behold, a sower went forth to sow; And when he sowed, some seeds fell by the way side, and the fowls came and devoured them up: Some fell upon stony places, where they had not much earth: and forthwith they sprung up, because they had no deepness of earth: And when the sun was up, they were scorched; and because they had no root, they withered away. And some fell among thorns; and the thorns sprung up, and choked them: But other fell into good ground, and brought forth fruit, some an hundredfold, some sixtyfold, some thirtyfold. Who hath ears to hear, let him hear.
— Matthew 13:3-9

As we can see, only one of the four seeds bears fruit. But what a fruit it is! A hundredfold! Similarly, the situation with followers looks the same. You can do everything right, and even more, but that doesn't guarantee that all your clients will become your followers! Some might not be in the right mood, others may be focused on other things, some might be preoccupied…

Using the example of a café, I'll share a model about followers that aligns with Jesus' parable.

GUEST:

Business: new clients, random buyers, website or physical store/venue visitors

Non-profit: recipients of humanitarian aid, parishioners of the community

Most often, everything starts with satisfying basic needs. In the case of a café, this could be the need to energize (caffeine), spend time in a cozy place, or hold a meeting, while ensuring the bill is not too high — affordable prices are key. A person who is fulfilling their basic needs is categorized as a **Guest.** The distinguishing feature of such customers is that they typically visit from time to time, make minimal purchases, and usually don't pay attention to recommending your establishment to their circle. In the case of a café, this could be due to factors like living or working far from the café, a preference for the taste of drinks or dishes at other places, availability of seats, service, etc.

A customers can remain in the **Guests** status for a long time unless something happens that moves them to the status of a **Regulars**.

REGULAR:

Business: royal customers, regular buyers, participants in loyalty programs;

Non-profit: recipients of humanitarian aid who show initiative and help organize events, active participants in the life of the church community.

Unlike a **Guest,** a **Regular** comes to the café with a clear purpose. He is loyal and open to trying something new. On average, he spends more compared to a **Guest**. Furthermore, a **Regular** arranges meetings at the café, thus promoting it to his acquaintances. The transition from a Guest to a Regular is facilitated by the realization that even their "basic need" can be satisfied in a unique way! In other words, it's about a so-called "Unique Selling Proposition"!

The Unique Selling Proposition (USP), also called the unique selling point or the unique value proposition (UVP) in the business model canvas, is the marketing strategy of informing customers about how one's own brand or product is superior to its competitors (in addition to its other values). (Wikipedia)

In the case of the café, this could include drinks made from exclusive coffee varieties, signature desserts, or the interior design. When a customer receives something that not only satisfies their needs and matches the money they've spent but also gives them a sense of exclusivity and being chosen among other options, it creates a unique experience. This is often associated with a feeling of exhilaration, comparable to the sensation when a magician reveals the secret behind their trick! Your reaction: "Wow! Incredible!"

FOLLOWER OR ADVOCATE:

Business: VIP clients, corporate clients, strategic partners;

Non-profit: recipients of humanitarian aid who have become full-fledged employees of your organization; leaders of the church community.

The next category of clients is the **Follower** or **Advocate**! Just like a real lawyer in court, these clients defend your interests and are essentially your freelance employees! Continuing with the café example, these clients not only intentionally come to you or schedule meetings at your café, but they also recommend drinks and dishes, and even treat other participants at the meeting! They can also tell others about your unique selling proposition! They often take a piece of your culture into their living environment — buying coffee beans and your desserts/dishes to take home or to the office, continuing to promote your establishment!

Typically, an **Advocate** is a **Regular** or, less often, a **Guest** who not only realizes that they are getting their needs met in a unique way but has also experienced certain impressions that can be described as "exchange with surplus"! This kind of exchange makes the customer feel gratitude, and they subconsciously want to tell many of their acquaintances how much they enjoyed your place and continue coming with their colleagues or friends. People generally seek to restore exchange to a balanced state by giving something in return. Thus, a grateful and satisfied client will recommend your product/service to everyone and will demonstrate loyalty to you! This increases your income level and reduces advertising costs, which should attract new customers.

FOOD FOR THOUGHT:

Reflecting on clients from this perspective, I noticed that this approach surprisingly aligns with the structure of God's Tabernacle:

Guests — this corresponds to the Outer Court. The Outer Court symbolizes clients who are in the initial stage of interaction with the company and have access to basic products and services. These clients can use the company's basic offerings, participate in promotions, and receive general information about products and services.

Regulars — this corresponds to the Inner Court or the Holy Place. The Holy Place symbolizes clients who have passed the initial stage of interaction with the company and are at a deeper level of engagement. These clients receive more personalized experience, can participate in specialized events, and have access to exclusive offers. They may also receive additional information and support.

Followers or Advocates — this corresponds to the Holy of Holies. The Holy of Holies symbolizes the most valuable and significant clients of the company, who have exceptional access to the highest quality and premium offerings. These clients receive individual service, access to unique products and services, personal managers, special events, and exclusive privileges.

Next, we will take a detailed look at customer categories and how it is possible to move customers from one category to another, ultimately aiming to guide the maximum number of customers to the category of **Followers or Advocates.**

The Third Leg of the Tabouret Principle: the Followers — Guest

Guest — a person entertained in one's house; a person to whom hospitality is extended; a person who pays for the services of an establishment (such as a hotel or restaurant).

If you can confidently answer "yes" to the statements below, it means that this component of successful teamwork and partnerships is implemented to some degree in your project:

- As part of the project, you have thoroughly described your target audience and its needs. On a regular basis, you conduct a review of the target audience and their needs.

- You possess information about similar offerings from competitors (other organizations) and you have an understanding that your offering is on par with what exists in the market.

But the stranger that dwelleth with you shall be unto you as one
born among you, and thou shalt love him as thyself; for ye were
strangers in the land of Egypt: I am the LORD your God.
— Leviticus 19:34

Be not forgetful to entertain strangers: for thereby some have
entertained angels unawares.
— Hebrews 13:2

God places a special emphasis on hospitality. The Bible describes situations involving the welcoming of guests who turned out to be angels of God (Abraham, Lot, Jacob, Joshua, Gideon, Mary, the shepherds, Peter...). Who knows, perhaps similar encounters have occurred in our lives, which we will only learn about when we reach Heaven?! Regardless, our Heavenly Father calls us to care for others as we care for ourselves.

Given that every guest has the potential to become a Follower-Advocate, it is critically important to avoid treating guests in a condescending manner based solely on their appearance or other external signs. The Bible repeatedly mentions that God is impartial! This is addressed in James' letter in the second chapter, where guests are seated based on their outward appearance. Moreover, sometimes organizations spend advertising budgets to attract customers, only for them to leave disappointed because they weren't given enough attention! Wise people say, "You never get a second chance to make a good first impression." Or, as another saying goes, a first impression is like pouring concrete: if something is done poorly, fixing it requires using a jackhammer to remove the previous layer!

FOOD FOR THOUGHT

In the course of a project selling massage equipment, I've often heard stories from colleagues about how misleading a customer's external appearance can be. Quite often, people with big jewelry, dressed in branded clothes, holding a briefcase or large wallet, would show a keen interest in the equipment, try various massagers, express their excitement, and sometimes behave arrogantly... only to end up buying nothing. At the same time, when the team saw such visitors, there was a subconscious expectation that because they looked "wealthy," they would definitely make a purchase. :)))

Meanwhile, many times, people dressed modestly, who reacted calmly to the massage effect, after trying the most expensive massager (a massage chair costing several thousand dollars), would either pay immediately or leave a deposit and arrange for delivery.

To do everything correctly, let's remember what lies at the core of relationships? Correct, it's the satisfaction of needs. A reward arises when one party offers to meet the needs of the other party in some way. To understand what specific needs we need to satisfy and how, it's important to describe the target audience.

The following few steps will help you describe your target audience:

1) GENERAL INFORMATION ABOUT YOUR TARGET AUDIENCE

To define your target audience, start by identifying their demographic characteristics, such as: age, gender, marital status, education, income level, and place of residence.

Next, you need to create an Empathy Map — the approach which is very well described in the book, written by Alexander Osterwalder and Yves Pigneur: "Business Model Generation "A Handbook for Visionaries, Game Changers, and Challengers". An Empathy Map helps to understand how your target audience perceives the world around them, what their experiences are, what they want, and what they fear. This is a highly useful tool in marketing, product design, and in developing products or services that meet real human needs. Moreover, it enables communication with the target audience in a language and terms that are clear and relatable to them.

To create an Empathy Map, imagine yourself as a representative of your target audience and answer the following questions:

a. What do they see around? What does the environment of your target audience look like? What brands and products are they observing around them? How do they perceive the situation in their field of activity (e.g., in business or work)?

b. What do they hear? What are the main sources of information the person receives (friends, family, colleagues, media)? What do they hear from people they trust (e.g., do they hear positive reviews about a certain product or service)?

c. What do they think and feel? What are the person's main concerns, worries and doubts? What are their dreams, aspirations and desires? What do they really want? How do they feel about their life or work? What inspires them?

d. What do I say and do? How does the person express their thoughts and feelings? What actions do they take based on their beliefs? How does this manifest in their behavior or actions?

The answer to these questions can bring you closer to understanding what is commonly referred to as the "pain point," meaning understanding the problems or challenges that prevent your target audience from achieving their goals or satisfying their needs. What do they fear? What frustrates or annoys them?

Perhaps, instead of the "pain point," it might be more beneficial to describe your target audience's needs as the "point of satisfaction," meaning understanding what your target audience strives for, what can bring them joy, satisfaction, and success. How do they define their "victory"? What changes in their life or work would they like to see? What will make them happy?

For better understanding and representation of your target audience, you can even create visual representations of them (infographics or diagrams). The better you understand your target audience, the better you can understand their needs, and as a result, the better satisfy them!

2) HOW DOES YOUR TARGET AUDIENCE INTERACT WITH YOUR PRODUCT OR SERVICE?

a. Purchase frequency: How often does your target audience use your product or service? It could be daily (like brushing teeth or drinking coffee), weekly (like reading a weekly publication or attending Sunday services at church), monthly (like purchasing laundry products or paying utility bills), etc.

b. Purchase motives: What are the main factors that drive people when making purchasing decisions? Is it the price? Quality? Recommendation?

c. Purchase channels: Online, through websites or social media, or offline, where people physically visit your location? How do they search for and determine where to make their purchases?

To gather all the necessary information about your target audience, typically, a combination of common sense, internal data, and direct interaction with the representatives of your target audience is enough.

Internal data refers to what you can observe by watching who and what is being bought from you. If you have a physical location, you can observe this firsthand. You can also use data from your order management system and loyalty programs. Additionally, if you manage social media accounts, analyzing who follows you and how they react to your posts can provide valuable insights. And of course, if you have a website, analyzing visitor information and activity can also be helpful.

As for interaction, I recommend paying attention to the following tools:

a. **Surveys:** The main goal is to collect quantitative data that can be easily analyzed. Questions are formulated in such a way that responses are short and structured: multiple-choice options, rating scales, or simply "yes" or "no." Surveys are usually conducted through questionnaires, online forms, or automated systems. It is effective when you need to quickly gather information from a large group of people.

b. **Selective interviews:** Since interviews are personal conversations that allow for deep and detailed answers, they are used when you need to understand not just a person's opinion, but their motivations, feelings, and experience. Unlike surveys, the questions here may change depending on the respondent's answers. Interviews are most often conducted orally — during face-to-face meetings, by phone, or online.

c. **Focus groups:** This research method involves engaging a small group of people (usually 6–10 participants) to discuss specific topics. The discussion is led by a moderator whose job is to encourage interaction among participants — people should start exchanging thoughts, sometimes debating or building on each other's ideas. Focus groups help to understand not only people's opinions but also the reasons behind them. Emotions, reactions, and nuances that are hard to identify through surveys or interviews can be observed here. Focus groups are often used in marketing, product development, advertising, and social research.

By describing your target audience through all these steps, you will better understand how to interact with your potential clients, which products or services to offer them, and which marketing and communication channels to use to achieve the best results. It is important to note that the information about the target audience should be reviewed from time to time and updated if any changes are detected!

FOOD FOR THOUGHT

Numerous studies on consumer behavior confirm that the deciding factors in whether to buy a product or service or not are the so-called EMO factors. EMO stands for EMO-tions. The key emotions that drive purchases are as follows:

- Fear: If you remember the advertisements of many medical products (and not only), you will understand that the main emotion the advertiser aims to provoke is fear for oneself or loved ones! If there's fear, action must be taken, meaning buying the advertised product!

- Pride: In this case, the idea is pushed that you will only have success or be respected by others when you own a product of a specific brand or use a particular service in a specific place. Many people, unfortunately, forget the known saying: "Don't judge a book by its cover" and pay too much focus to their appearance, forgetting to back it up with thoughtful conversations and actions.

- Greed: How about an offer of products or services with discounts of 30%, 50%, or even 90%? Or the proposal to buy two products for the price of one? I don't know about you, but I've always had a hard time resisting such offers, especially if it's a product or item I already use.

- Love: Love is also a powerful motivator for purchases. If you love someone, you'll definitely buy it! A person who wants to express their love won't stop at much! Jewelry, flowers, medicine, sweets, other food items, and goods — many advertisers focus on love to "reach" the wallets of potential buyers.

- Conscience: Are you concerned about ecology? Global warming? Perhaps something on the level of your city? Conscience can also drive purchases. Refusing plastic bags and disposable plastic tableware, choosing products from companies that implement environmentally friendly technologies, donating to charity projects when buying certain goods or services — all these are examples of how this emo-factor works.

These five emotions are key from a marketing perspective and are the most commonly used in advertising goods or services.

Reflective task:

Taking into account the information received, conduct a review of your target audience description. See if there are any additional related needs that you could also address.

The next step is to conduct a comparative analysis of alternative or competitive offerings. Performing a competitive analysis allows you to understand your business's current position in the market, identify competitors' strengths and weaknesses, and determine how you can improve your offering to ensure it is at least as good as, if not better than, your competitors'. Below is a step-by-step algorithm for conducting a competitive analysis. I recommend that you create a table and input all the information you gather.

Identify your competitors.

Create a complete list of competitors. Identify both direct competitors (those offering similar products or services) and indirect competitors (those offering alternative products or services that meet the same customer needs) in your industry.

Collect information about your competitors.

Official sources and social media: competitor websites, press releases, price lists, brochures, competitor activity on social media platforms (Facebook, Instagram, LinkedIn, etc.).

Customer reviews: analyze feedback on various platforms, such as Google Reviews and others.

Feedback from customers and employees: surveys and interviews with customers and employees in your company who may have experience of interacting with competitors.

Visiting retail locations: visit competitors' physical stores (if available).

Analyze competitive factors and compare the obtained information with your products or services.

Comparative analysis of products, services, and prices: Evaluate the product and service range of competitors. Compare quality, unique features, and innovations. Study the packaging and presentation of products. Compare competitors' prices with yours. Investigate the presence of discounts, promotions, and loyalty programs. Assess the price/quality ratio.

Marketing strategies: Study the marketing channels used by competitors (online, offline, social media, email marketing, etc.). Analyze advertising campaigns, content marketing, and PR activities. Evaluate the competitors' presence on social media and their interaction with audiences.

Customer service analysis: Evaluate the quality of customer service, including pre- and post-sales service. Investigate strategies for handling complaints and returns. Study the warranties and return policies offered.

Online presence analysis: Review competitors' websites in terms of design, usability, informativeness, and functionality. Analyze competitors' SEO rankings and the quality of content on their sites. Evaluate the availability of mobile applications.

Conduct a comparative analysis of competitors: Identify the key strengths and weaknesses of each competitor. Identify potential areas for improvement and growth for your business, as well as potential threats. Summarize the information obtained and draw conclusions about the current position of your offering in the market. Use the data to adjust your marketing strategy and differentiate your offering from competitors.

Monitoring Changes

Continuous Monitoring: Regularly update information about competitors and analyze their activities. Make adjustments to strategies based on new data and market changes.

Evaluation of Results: Assess the effectiveness of implemented changes and their impact on your project. Regularly conduct re-analysis to maintain the relevance of your strategies.

Competitive analysis allows you to gain a deeper understanding of the market in which you operate and identify ways to improve your competitiveness.

By conducting these two actions — describing your target audience and analyzing your competitors — you will be able to shape an offering that best addresses people's needs while taking into account other market propositions!

Reflective task:

Based on the obtained information, conduct a comparative analysis of competitive/alternative offerings. Look at where and how your offer can be improved!

The Third Leg of The Tabouret Principle: the Followers — Regular

Regular (from Late Latin regularis regular, from Latin, regula — rule) — one who is regular; one who is usually present or participating; one who can be trusted or depended on.

If you can confidently answer "yes" to the statements below, it means that this component of successful work is, to some extent, implemented in your project:

- All that is mentioned for the Guest

- You have one or more Unique Selling Proposition that stand out favorably among other similar offerings.

And a great multitude followed him, because they saw his miracles which he did on them that were diseased.
— John 6:2

Each of the four Gospels contains descriptions of the miracles that Jesus performed. Large crowds followed Jesus because they saw how He healed and fed people. Even though they were not fully prepared to accept His teaching and become His followers, they could receive healing or food, which attracted them to Him to the extent that they actively sought Him out!

The **Regular** level implies a relationship model based on the recognition of the uniqueness of a product or service that helps satisfy a basic need! Unfortunately, the vast majority of projects offer more or less similar products or services at more or less similar prices. They often see competitive advantage as the ability to sell something cheaper. However, this is something that is relatively easy to copy, and such an advantage is not sustainable! If someone lowers the price of a product or service or introduces a new product or service into their lineup, other sellers quickly catch on, which soon eliminates the advantage.

A Unique Selling Proposition, also called a Sustainable Competitive Advantage, is what helps the client understand that they are receiving something valuable in exchange for their effort or money — something that sets you apart from other similar or alternative offerings in the long term!

FOOD FOR THOUGHT

There are many coffee shops that, under the guise of coffee, sell a dark brown liquid with a specific bitter taste that is hard to drink without a large dose of sugar or milk. In contrast, you might offer a drink of an entirely different level—with a bright, amazing aroma and a rich, full-bodied flavor. How is that possible?

Because you've invested time and effort to source and purchase high-quality, freshly roasted specialty Arabica coffee beans, adjust the grind and coffee machine settings properly, and train your staff (baristas) to perfection!

Even though the price for a cup of coffee is more or less the same everywhere, for a **Regular**, it becomes clear why they choose this coffee shop over another. At another place, they might pay a little less but receive something mediocre. At this coffee shop, the **Regular** will pay more but receive something that fully matches the value of their spending.

The idea of creating Unique Selling Points (Sustainable Competitive Advantages) is very well explained in the book "Blue Ocean Strategy" by W. Chan Kim and Renée Mauborgne. They compare the competitive environment to a "red ocean" and the situation where you have a Unique Selling Points (Sustainable Competitive Advantages) to a "blue ocean."

Why is the ocean "red"? Because it is filled with competitors — sharks — that bite each other, making the ocean red with blood. These "bites" represent the practice of selling products at a discount. Profit for a business plays the same role as blood for the body. Just as blood delivers oxygen and nutrients to every cell, profit allows a company to maintain and upgrade its infrastructure, improve its products or services, and hire the best employees. Every time you sell products or services at a discount, you are essentially bleeding yourself. The funds you lose on the discount could have been used for updates, growth, and scaling. Instead, both you and your competitors are simply selling products or services for less.

So, what exactly is the "blue" ocean? A blue ocean is a situation where there is little or no competition. Thanks to your Unique Selling Points (Sustainable Competitive Advantages), it becomes difficult or even impossible for your customers to compare the price of your product or service with similar offerings on the market. As a result, they can easily justify to themselves why they are willing to pay the price you are asking. For them, it makes perfect sense. "Yes, I could buy something similar elsewhere for less, but it would only be 'similar,' not exactly what I want!"

Therefore, the key question you need to answer is: What do people truly need that is currently missing from the market and that no one else has yet offered? Ideally, it's not just about improving an existing product — it's about creating something that people genuinely need but that doesn't exist yet!

A great example of this is the circus industry. Most circuses rely on traditional acts with animals, acrobats, jugglers, and clowns... The competition is intense. But one circus stands out — "Cirque du Soleil" (Canada). Unlike most competitors, "Cirque du Soleil" abandoned animal acts and the typical format where performers simply rotate through acts. Instead, they created a true circus theater — with a storyline, music, and, of course, spectacular performances!

Rather than fighting for the existing audience, they created an entirely new one. The result? "Cirque du Soleil" shows have been successful in over 300 cities worldwide, with over 150 million attendees!

So, how do you find your own "Blue Ocean"? If you've already completed the task of describing your target audience at the "Guest" level and clearly understand whose needs — and which ones — your project is meeting, it will be much easier to identify or articulate your unique and sustainable advantage.

Start by looking at what you do from a different perspective. Ask yourself: What frustrates people about this industry? What problems or inconveniences do customers face? Could something be done more simply, more quickly, more affordably — or in a way that's just plain cooler?

Typically, the answers to these questions revolve around four strategic directions, which form the ERRC matrix (Eliminate–Reduce–Raise–Create):

1. What Can Be Eliminated? (Eliminate)

Sometimes your product or service may include elements that increase costs but provide no real value to customers — or simply exist "out of habit." Can you remove such elements to reduce your expenses?

a. Replace a traditional cashier with app or terminal payments. This would eliminate queues, reduce cashier payroll expenses, and create a new customer experience through interactive payment options.

b. Reduce a large menu of drinks or food and focus on a few unique signature offerings that set you apart from competitors. This would lower costs for materials and reduce waste while improving the quality and speed of preparation — since you'd be perfecting a smaller number of items instead of managing a complex menu.

c. Instead of expensive annual gym memberships that people buy but rarely use, offer more flexible attendance options. This would make your service more affordable and create additional comfort and convenience for customers.

Reflective task:

Based on the information obtained, suggest Elimination actions related to your product or service.

2. What Can Be Reduced? (Reduce)

Unlike the first option, here we're talking about reducing costs on certain elements of your product or service that are important, but not the primary reason for the purchase!

a. Allow customers to register on your website themselves. This reduces administrative costs associated with entering customer information into your database, generating invoices, and monitoring payments.

b. Instead of personal trainers in a fitness club, implement AI assistants. This could lower costs while creating a new experience for clients. A similar approach could be applied in other business areas, such as organizing travel tours!

c. Instead of long training courses that take months, offer an "intensive" that lasts a few weeks or days! Additionally, replacing tests with real-world tasks creates an environment where students can practically apply what they've learned.

Reflective task:

Based on the information obtained, suggest Reductive actions related to your product or service.

3. What Can Be Raised? (Raise)

In this context, we are talking about strengthening your competitive advantages and creating higher value for customers in areas that are critically important to them! Make these aspects better than your competitors.

a. For a coffee shop, the barista plays a crucial role — not just in preparing drinks, but in engaging with guests. If you train your team not only in making high-quality coffee drinks but also in excellent communication skills, you can significantly enhance your establishment's appeal!

b. For a car service business, you can create a cozy waiting room and offer coffee, internet access, etc. You could also introduce warranties on your services, operate 24/7, or provide convenient evening hours.

c. For an educational services business, you could implement elements of learning through games (gamification) — such as quests, rankings, and rewards for achieving results. Gamification typically increases participant engagement in the process and outcome. Forming teams will add an additional incentive for participants to be more active and reach the end goal!

Reflective task:

Based on the information obtained, suggest Araisive actions related to your product or service.

4. What Can Be Created? (Create)

In this case, the goal is to introduce new elements that are absent or rare in the market. Something that can become a true "signature" of your company, something your competitors don't offer. A new approach, technology, service, or format.

a. For a coffee shop, this could be creating a unique coffee-serving ritual that guests will remember for a long time.

b. For a fitness club, it could be implementing virtual zones where people can exercise in a virtual environment, such as "running in Paris" or "cycling through the Alps".

c. For a toy store, it could be adding a toy rental service — parents can rent toys for a certain period, paying for the rental, and after a month or so, when the child loses interest in the toy, they can exchange it for a new one.

Reflective task:

Based on the information obtained, suggest Creative actions related to your product or service.

FOOD FOR THOUGHT

It's interesting that the world's largest taxi service provider, Uber, doesn't own a single car (at least at the beginning)! The world's largest property rental operator, Airbnb, doesn't own any apartments! These companies are prime examples of how to create a "blue ocean" by combining options from the ERRC matrix.

If you take a closer look, both of these companies eliminated unnecessary elements, like communication with operators, and added ratings, reviews, and convenient payment options. By not copying your competitors but instead trying to combine something that hasn't been done before, you can surely create your own "blue ocean"!

Track trends and understand what people like. Test ideas on a small audience before scaling them up. Stay flexible – because the "blue ocean" is constantly changing!

Finally, I want to share successful examples of well-known companies that have managed to find their "blue oceans" and built their Unique Selling Points (Sustainable Competitive Advantages) around them:

Product or Service

Apple: The company is known for its high-quality, innovative design of its devices: iPhone, MacBook, iPad, iMac... Apple products not only combine cutting-edge technology with sleek design, creating a strong emotional response in users, but they are unified into a single ecosystem through the iOS operating system, iCloud cloud storage, and other apps.

Dyson: Known for its high-quality household appliances like vacuum cleaners and hairdryers. Dyson products feature innovative solutions and durability.

Bose: A leader in audio equipment manufacturing, Bose is known for its high-quality sound and innovations in noise-canceling technology.

Personalized Approach to Customers

Zappos: An online shoe and clothing retailer, known for its top-notch customer service. Zappos is famous for offering free shipping for multiple sizes, so customers can choose the best fit, and free returns for items that don't fit.

Four Seasons Hotels: A premium hotel chain where the primary focus is personalized service and creating a tailored experience for every guest.

Innovation and Technology

Tesla: Tesla stands out for its cutting-edge technologies in electric vehicles, autonomous driving, and battery manufacturing. Their innovative solutions in these areas have made Tesla a market leader in electric cars.

Spotify: A music streaming platform that revolutionized the music industry with its user-friendly interface, customization options, and recommendation algorithms.

Zoom: A video conferencing service that became extremely popular due to its ease of use, high-quality video, and scalability for various needs, from individuals to large organizations.

Unique Business Model

Airbnb: A platform for renting accommodations that has transformed the tourism industry by offering users unique lodging options worldwide and allowing hosts to rent out their own homes and apartments.

Uber: A taxi service platform that provides quick, convenient, and affordable transportation solutions for people worldwide. The easy-to-use app and transparent pricing system have made Uber a popular choice.

Netflix: With its revolutionary streaming model, Netflix changed the entertainment industry. They provide users with access to a large library of movies and TV series via a monthly subscription, which turned out to be more convenient and affordable compared to traditional cable TV and video rentals.

Exclusivity and Status

Rolex: Rolex watches are considered a symbol of status and prestige. The company focuses on producing high-quality, exclusive timepieces that give owners a sense of elitism.

Hermès: A French company known for its luxury goods, including bags, clothing, and accessories. Hermès is famous for its craftsmanship, materials, and prestige.

Bentley: A manufacturer of luxury cars that are associated with exclusivity, luxury, and high social status.

Ecology and Sustainability

Ikea: The company actively promotes environmentally sustainable materials and practices in its production and business. They also offer furniture return and recycling programs.

TOMS Shoes: A footwear company known for its "One for One" program, where for every pair of shoes sold, the company donates a pair to someone in need. This is a social responsibility and sustainability effort across the supply chain.

Convenience, Accessibility, Location

Amazon: Amazon offers a vast selection of products with fast and reliable delivery. The convenience of use and the wide range of options make Amazon the preferred choice for many shoppers.

Walmart: Known for its low prices and wide selection of goods. Walmart provides affordable prices and convenient access to essential products for millions of customers.

FOOD FOR THOUGHT

In the economy and society at large, the so-called "Pareto Principle," or the "80/20 Rule," is quite common. It suggests that 20% of efforts bring 80% of the results. In a broad sense, this ratio emphasizes the non-linearity of efforts and outcomes. That is, there are certain areas of activity where your contribution will have a larger impact on achieving the desired result compared to others. In business, it's often observed that: 20% of customers bring in 80% of the profits; or 20% of your product range accounts for 80% of sales; or 20% of mistakes in the process cause 80% of problems. The Pareto Principle is named after the Italian economist and sociologist Vilfredo Pareto, who, while studying the distribution of real estate among the population in Italy, concluded that about 80% of the property was owned by just 20% of the population.

What is the practical application of the Pareto Principle? First and foremost, you need to clearly understand and identify this key 20% that has the greatest impact on the result. For example, you have certain products or services that you offer to clients. Determine what percentage of the total revenue each of them contributes to the compan's total income. Organize these products in descending order of their share. Create a separate column and start adding these shares cumulatively: add the second share to the first, then add the third share to the sum of the first two, and so on, until you have added all the shares and the total is 100%! Through this exercise, you will see which top positions contribute 80% of the revenue! Going forward, in everything you do or plan to do, you need to pay special attention to the top positions because their impact on your results is the greatest! Cutting costs or increasing revenue for one or more top positions will have a significantly larger impact on the overall result compared to similar changes for the remaining positions!

Reflective task:

Based on the information obtained, identify and write down your Unique Selling (Sustainable) Propositions.

Review how your target audience can learn about or experience your Unique Selling (Sustainable) Propositions.

Apply Pareto principle to your case and identify top 20% of your portfolio.

The Third Leg of the Tabouret Principle: the Followers - Advocate

Advocate (from Latin advocātus, noun derivative from past participle of advocāre "to summon, call to one's aid,") — one who defends or maintains a cause or proposal; one who supports or promotes the interests of a cause or group.

If you can confidently answer "yes" to the statements below, it means that this component of successful work is, to some extent, implemented in your project:

- Everything mentioned for the Guest and the Regular.

- You have an understanding and implementation of the elements of the "Experience Economy."

And Enoch lived sixty and five years, and begat Methuselah: And Enoch walked with God after he begat Methuselah three hundred years, and begat sons and daughters: And all the days of Enoch were three hundred sixty and five years: And Enoch walked with God: and he was not; for God took him.
— Genesis 5:21-24

But Noah found grace in the eyes of the LORD. These are the generations of Noah: Noah was a just man and perfect in his generations, and Noah walked with God.
— Genesis 6:8-9

Now the LORD had said unto Abram, Get thee out of thy country, and from thy kindred, and from thy father's house, unto a land that I will shew thee: And I will make of thee a great nation, and I will bless thee, and make thy name great; and thou shalt be a blessing: And I will bless them that bless thee, and curse him that curseth thee: and in thee shall all families of the earth be blessed. So Abram departed, as the LORD had spoken unto him; and Lot went with him: and Abram was seventy and five years old when he departed out of Haran.
— Genesis 12:1-4

And when he had found him, he brought him unto Antioch. And it came to pass, that a whole year they assembled themselves with the church, and taught much people. And the disciples were called Christians first in Antioch.
— Acts 11:26

Both the Old and New Testaments are filled with examples of true followers of God: Abel, Enoch, Noah, Abraham, Isaac, Jacob, Joseph, Moses, David, Mary, John the Baptist, the Apostles, and many others. What set them apart from the rest of the people, who were often satisfied with miracles of healing and the multiplication of bread? Unlike the common crowd, each of these true followers faced various life challenges — sometimes even threats to their very lives. Yet they made their choice and, in most cases, remained faithful to it no matter what. Why?

Everything created by the Lord is created with a purpose. No matter what you focus on, every little detail plays a role in the structure of the universe. The stars provide light at night, help with navigation, and serve as signs. The sun gives warmth and light. Air, water, earth, animals, and plants — all have their place and purpose.

If we consider humanity, we see that when the Creator forms each of us, He places within us His will — a unique role and purpose that we are called to discover and fulfill throughout our lives. This can be compared to a children's game where you match shapes to the correct openings. A square or triangular piece won't fit into a round hole — only a round piece will fit. Similarly, when you encounter something in life that aligns with your calling or higher purpose, you intuitively feel deep within, "Yes, this is it." It's the very reason worth living for.

This inner sense serves as both a sail and an anchor for you. It acts as a sail by inspiring you to move forward and as an anchor by grounding you when you face life's storms and difficult situations — keeping you from giving up. If you don't discover this sense of purpose, you may experience a kind of inner despair, a feeling of frustration — a gap between where you are and where you're meant to be. Unfortunately, some people who fail to find this purpose may end their lives in despair. But those who discover it live truly meaningful lives and leave behind "fruit that remains."

When we talked about the second leg of the Tabouret — specifically about "Wanting" — we explored Maslow's Hierarchy of Needs. There's a parallel between the levels of Maslow's Pyramid and the types of clients you serve.

Guests correspond to the first level — the satisfaction of physiological needs. They are primarily focused on meeting basic needs and aren't concerned with anything beyond that.

Regulars align with the second, third, and fourth levels — Safety, Belonging, and Esteem. They seek high-quality products or services that meet their expectations and deliver consistent value. Regulars are aware that other options exist and that trying them might result in unpleasant surprises, so they prefer to stick with a trusted option. They are usually familiar with your company's staff, appreciate personal attention from employees, and enjoy a sense of social connection when engaging with your product or service. A loyalty program or a VIP card enhances their sense of status and makes them feel valued compared to other customers.

Followers or Advocates correspond to the fifth level — Self-Actualization, which reflects a person's desire to reach their full potential and maximize their abilities and talents. In the context of a product or service, this means that clients receive a unique and transformative experience that generates deep loyalty and enthusiasm toward your offer. As a result, they don't just remain loyal followers themselves — they actively promote your brand to their friends and family. They genuinely believe that other alternatives are not as good and sincerely want their friends to have the best experience possible!

How can you create this unique experience?

To move a client from the status of a **Regular** to the status of a **Follower or Advocate**, you need to create what is called a "value exchange with surplus." In other words, you need to "wow" your client or provide something that, in their eyes, holds greater value than the price they are paying for the product or service.

One of the most effective ways to implement this "value exchange with surplus" is through the concept of the "Experience Economy" proposed by Joseph Pine and James Gilmore. This theory suggests that businesses no longer simply sell products or services — they create complete and memorable experiences for their clients.

To illustrate this concept, let's take a look at coffee.

COFFEE AS A RAW MATERIAL

Did you know that the coffee tree is a very delicate plant? Factors like humidity levels, air temperature, sunlight, soil, and protection from pests all have a significant impact on the yield and flavor of coffee beans! Moreover, coffee trees often grow on mountain slopes, which means that taking care of them requires not only advanced techniques but also great dedication and attention.

Coffee cherries resemble regular cherries, and the coffee bean is essentially like the pit of a cherry. Farmers need to carefully separate the pulp from the bean, dry it, and only then can it be sold. The price of commercial-grade green coffee (Arabica and Robusta) ranges from $2 to $10 per kilogram. Let's take the average — about $5 per kilogram.

Even though green coffee is the key ingredient for creating an aromatic and flavorful beverage — as the saying goes, "cheap fish makes bad soup" — enjoying a delicious cup of coffee requires much more effort! You need to transport it, roast it, grind it, and finally brew it… That's why the value of green coffee remains relatively low despite its essential role.

COFFEE AS A COMMODITY

Various companies that produce roasted and instant coffee, such as Nestlé (brand Nescafé) or Mondelez (brands Jacobs, Carte Noire), buy green beans, roast them, and then either package the roasted whole beans, grind them, or process them into instant coffee. Roasted coffee, whether whole beans or ground, typically costs between $10 and $20 per kilogram, while instant coffee is around $50 per kilogram. This results in an average price of processed green beans being around $30 to $35 per kilogram.

It's clear that coffee as a product is more expensive than green coffee because you need to put in minimal additional effort to enjoy the beverage. Simply heat water and add the grounded coffee to a container or coffee maker. After a few minutes, your drink is ready!

FOOD FOR THOUGHT:

For me, instant coffee is like "second-hand" clothes. It's already been brewed once. In the process of making instant coffee, it is brewed, then the water is evaporated through various methods, leaving behind a concentrate. This concentrate almost has no aroma and, at the same time, has a mediocre taste — essential oils that give coffee its distinctive notes of flavor and aroma are irreversibly lost during the thermal processing of the raw material. Given this, manufacturers use the cheapest beans for its production. Of course, there are places where instant coffee is a necessity (such as on hikes or at the front). But if you want to truly enjoy coffee, I recommend choosing only whole bean coffee of the Arabica variety (even better, Specialty Arabica) with a roasting date no more than 30-45 days from the purchase date. Why? Because Arabica generally has a more distinctive aroma and flavor compared to Robusta, and Specialty Arabica, thanks to the unique conditions in which the coffee trees are grown, has even more pronounced aroma and flavor!

As for the roasting date, just like bread becomes stale 2-3 days after baking, coffee beans lose 50% to 90% of their essential oils responsible for aroma and flavor within 45-60 days after roasting. And of course, coffee beans should be grounded just before brewing. Even if you store ground coffee in a vacuum-sealed package, it doesn't stop the loss of essential oils!

COFFEE AS A SERVICE

When you go to a café or any establishment and order a ready-made drink—whether it's an espresso, americano, cappuccino, or any other beverage—you're paying for the drink, not the coffee beans! Typically, 7-9 grams of ground coffee are used to make one serving of coffee. So, from one kilogram of coffee beans, you can prepare between 110 and 140 servings! The average cost of a cup of coffee in Ukraine is around $1 (black coffee may be slightly cheaper, and coffee with milk may cost more, and of course, Starbucks coffee would be priced higher). This means that the cost of coffee now amounts to about $120 per kilogram.

The increase in the cost of "coffee as a service" is linked to the additional service you receive. Unlike previous options, you don't have to do anything yourself. You just walk into the establishment and order your drink. Furthermore, the location of the café, the cozy interior, the specialized equipment, and the involvement of staff in preparing the beverage all contribute to the increased cost.

COFFEE AS AN EXPERIENCE (IMPRESSIONS)

I've been lucky enough to visit Venice a few times. Imagine this: you arrive at the train station — because you have to travel by train, since driving there poses a high risk of getting stuck in traffic — and immediately step into a magical atmosphere of celebration. Gondoliers in their signature striped shirts and wide-brimmed hats, the scent of the sea and food, many smiling people, incredibly charming little houses, conversations, music... You walk through narrow streets until you reach Piazza San Marco, where you get a view of the sea. On one side, there's the Church of Saint Mark. On the other sides the square is surrounded by old buildings with numerous arches. The square is filled with small tables where people usually drink coffee or other beverages while feeding pigeons. If you order a coffee, it will cost you 15-20 euros per serving! And they use the same 7-9g of ground coffee beans to prepare it! This means the cost of coffee per kilogram is roughly 2,000 dollars!

From my own experience, I would recommend ordering pizza or other food somewhere else in the city. Here, in the square, first of all, it's crowded with people, many pigeons, and the quality of the food might leave much to be desired (or maybe I just got unlucky with the place?). But if you've made it to the square, you'll naturally want to stay for a while to soak in the atmosphere.

This is why the vast majority of tourists here order coffee or other drinks and spend half an hour to an hour enjoying the sea, chatting with loved ones, and feeding the pigeons.

In summary, the same product — in our case, coffee — can be sold at prices ranging from $5 to $2,000 per kilogram! Sounds unbelievable? Yes. But what if I told you that there is a certain technique that can transform any place into a kind of "Venice"? The Experience Economy is all about how you can, even from Ukraine or anywhere else, create an outstanding experience and, accordingly, sell your products or services at a completely different price!

The foundation of this economy is based on four main components: **Education, Engagement, Escape from Reality, and Aesthetics**. Let's take a closer look at each of these elements.

1. EDUCATION

Customer Education is a key aspect of the Experience Economy. Education can be compared to how a magician, after performing a trick, explains to you the secret and how they perform the various maneuvers. Typically, this sparks admiration and a phrase like, "Wow!" It also automatically makes you a part of the small circle of those "initiated into the magic" of the trick!

Moreover, education has quite practical applications. For example, in a coffee shop, I can share that our "Advocates" are well-versed in coffee, and when they buy it at other coffee shops or prepare it themselves, they can control the quality of the drink to ensure maximum enjoyment! In a similar way, buying coffee for the office or home ceases to be a lottery — an "Advocate" knows what to look for and how to choose tasty coffee! They can consciously choose higher quality, albeit more expensive, varieties, understanding what they are paying for. Knowledge about coffee brings customers not only organoleptic and emotional pleasure. Understanding the history, creation process, and characteristics of their favorite drink adds depth and significance to their daily rituals. Visiting a coffee shop becomes a mindful enjoyment, not just a consumption of a drink. Studying coffee culture contributes to the development of taste receptors. Customers begin to distinguish the subtle flavor notes that depend on the origin of the beans, processing methods, roasting, and preparation of the drink. This makes the process of consuming coffee more captivating and rich in experiences. Furthermore, knowledge of coffee traditions from different countries, interaction with others, and expanding social connections broaden one's cultural outlook and allow them to feel part of the global coffee lovers' community.

Thus, Education not only satisfies the intellectual needs of customers but also creates deep and unforgettable experiences that contribute to their personal growth and strengthen their relationship with the brand. Customer enlightenment involves integrating educational components into services and products. It can include various forms of interaction that foster the acquisition of knowledge and skills. The main mechanisms of Education include:

- **Visual learning:** Elements of games and practical tasks contribute to better material absorption. For example, in a café or restaurant, you could place posters on the walls with information about coffee: its cultivation, processing and preparation, etc. Alternatively, you could use paper placemats under the dishes to display coffee-related information or use it as a crossword (puzzle) space on the topic of coffee, which customers can try to solve while waiting for their order. A similar approach can be seen in businesses related to massage equipment, where posters with the structure of the spine or joints are displayed.

- **Practical experience:** Learning through actions and solving specific tasks promotes better understanding and memory retention. Masterclasses and workshops are great examples of this method. For example, in our café, we regularly hosted tastings of exclusive coffee varieties, which were by invitation for our "Advocates." This not only helped to build positive brand associations but also created friendly relationships among visitors themselves.

- **Multimedia resources:** Using video, animation, virtual reality, and other multimedia technologies makes the learning process more engaging and accessible. In one wellness project, visitors to salons are offered the opportunity to watch animations about the physiological processes that occur in the body during the use of massage equipment. This helps visitors become more conscious of the benefits of using the equipment while also contributing to their well-being through psychosomatic processes.

Psychosomatics — of, relating to, concerned with, or involving both mind and body; of, relating to, involving, or concerned with bodily symptoms caused by mental or emotional disturbance.

- **Personalized learning process:** Adapting learning content according to the individual needs and interests of customers increases their motivation and learning effectiveness. In wellness projects, for example, consultants, by communicating personally with each visitor, would learn about specific health issues and requests for improvement. Based on this information, the consultant would then determine which equipment to use and how often, tailoring the experience to the individual's needs.

Reflective task:

Based on the information obtained, suggest actions which can Educate your Clients about your product or service or your company.

_____

_____

_____

_____

_____

_____

_____

_____

_____

2. ENGAGEMENT

Engagement plays one of the central roles in the Experience Economy, providing customers with immersion in unique and exciting experiences that go beyond the everyday routine. This aspect of interaction helps businesses create strong emotional bonds with customers, enhances their loyalty, and fosters long-term relationships.

Engagement works through active customer participation in the process of creating their own experience. It requires customers not only to be passive observers but also to actively interact with the surrounding environment, which offers them choice, creativity, and the opportunity to contribute to the final result. The main mechanisms of engagement include:

- **Interactive elements** that encourage customers to engage with the product or service are key to creating a more immersive experience. For example, visitors to an escape room solve puzzles and tasks to achieve the goal of escaping the room.

- **Creating a fully immersive experience** that captivates all of the customer's senses helps them completely dive into the experience. Virtual reality (VR) environments and theme parks are prime examples of such immersive environments.

- **Offering customers the ability to personalize their experience** further enhances engagement. Online games and educational platforms that adapt content to individual preferences demonstrate a high level of user engagement.

As a result, engagement allows customers to experience deep emotional experiences, leading to greater satisfaction with the acquired experience. It helps them feel a connection to the brand and enhances their emotional well-being. Engagement also gives customers the opportunity to express their creativity and uniqueness. This is an important aspect of self-realization that promotes personal growth and satisfaction. Active participation in learning processes makes the information acquisition process more effective and unforgettable.

In the case of coffee shops, whenever we work on a new menu, we try to include items that involve the customer in the preparation of the drink or dish, or its final touch in front of the customer. This way, customers feel involved and gain much more emotional value from the experience.

Reflective task:

Based on the information obtained, suggest actions which can Engage your Clients into interaction with your product or service or your company.

_____

_____

_____

_____

_____

_____

_____

_____

_____

_____

_____

3. ESCAPE FROM REALITY

Escape from Reality is another crucial component of the Experience Economy. This aspect of interaction focuses on providing customers with the opportunity to temporarily escape from their daily routine and stress into exciting worlds and situations. This is the foundation of the popularity of all video games and simulations. Just imagine, in real life you're a shy adolescent going through puberty, but in the game, you're a general, a leader, a conqueror! On top of that, you even have an avatar that reflects this — a fierce, muscular warrior in armor or something like that. Immersion in fantastic worlds and new contexts stimulates creative thinking and imagination, which can lead to the emergence of new ideas and solutions.

Providing customers with opportunities for enjoyment and satisfaction through immersive experiences increases their overall sense of life satisfaction. Escape from reality often involves collective activities, which help strengthen social bonds and create new friendships. For example, hosting themed events like carnivals or masquerades, where wearing a character costume is a must, allows visitors to transform and feel like someone else for the duration of the event! A temporary break from everyday tasks and problems helps customers recharge and restore their energy, which boosts their productivity and motivation going forward, as well as their loyalty to your brand. The most vivid examples of Escape from Reality in the experience economy include:

- **Virtual rooms and costume programs**, which transport visitors into different worlds, ranging from fantasy to historical settings.

- **Themed cafes, restaurants, and parks** stylized to reflect fantasy or historical eras. Some of the most spectacular examples are parks like Disneyland and Universal Studios.

- **Role-playing games** with a storyline that allow participants to transform into different characters. Examples include:

  - **Mafia** — an intellectual and psychological step-by-step role-playing game in the detective genre that models the battle between an organized minority and an unorganized majority.

  - **Monopoly and Rat Races** — popular board games aimed at developing financial literacy.

- **Charades** — a game originally created for diver training, where players must act out words through pantomime for others to guess.

Escape from reality plays a crucial role in creating a complete and inspiring customer experience. It is not just a form of entertainment, but also a powerful tool for improving the emotional and mental well-being of visitors. Companies that successfully create and promote escape-from-reality technologies can offer valuable emotional release and inspiration to their customers, which contributes to their long-term loyalty and satisfaction.

Reflective task:

Based on the information obtained, suggest actions somehow related to your product or service or your company which can help your Clients to Escape from Reality.

4. AESTHETICS

Aesthetics is an inseparable part of the Experience Economy. At its core, aesthetics is about creating environments and products that engage the senses (sight, hearing, smell, taste, touch), satisfy aesthetic needs, evoke emotions, and leave lasting impressions. Aesthetics helps clients enjoy the moment here and now, adding value and meaning to their experience.

Aesthetics works through the creation of vivid and attractive visual, auditory, taste, olfactory, and tactile experiences that enhance the overall impression of a product or service. The main mechanisms of this process include:

- **Sight:** The visual design of spaces, products, and packaging plays a crucial role in creating attractiveness and aesthetic appeal. Interior design and architectural features create a unique atmosphere that attracts customers and holds their attention. Additionally, it's essential to consider the cleanliness of the staff, the spaces, and the surrounding area, as well as the cleanliness of service vehicles — these all contribute to the visual perception of your product or service!

- **Hearing:** The sound accompaniment, including music and sound effects, enhances the emotional perception of space and experience. Therefore, it's important to select musical accompaniment that matches the profile of your target audience, avoiding unnecessary noise and sharp sounds.

- **Smell:** Scents associated with your product or service can either strengthen the emotional connection or, conversely, drive customers away! Agree, even if you have the best product, if it's carried by someone with the smell of sweat, it's not going to work!

- **Taste:** Even if your product or service has nothing to do with food, you should still create opportunities for your clients to taste something: coffee or tea, chocolate candies, snacks — these will enhance the positive impressions of your interaction with your product or service.

- **Touch:** The use of materials and textures that feel pleasant to the touch helps create positive tactile impressions. Velvet or suede instead of rough fabrics, comfortable tableware and utensils, packaging that's easy to open — these are just a few examples of how touch is used to enhance the customer experience.

As a result, aesthetics fulfill the need for beauty and harmony through visual and sensory elements, creating pleasant impressions and emotions that enhance the mood and overall well-being of customers, helping reduce stress and tension. Aesthetics leave bright and pleasant memories that strengthen the emotional connection between customers and the brand, encouraging them to return again. Companies that successfully integrate aesthetics into their products and services can expect a high level of customer satisfaction and loyalty, contributing to their long-term success and competitive advantage.

Each of these additions makes its unique contribution to creating a rich and unforgettable experience for customers, helping them transition from being just a Regular to a dedicated Follower-Advocate, and forming strong emotional bonds with them.

Reflective task:

Based on the information obtained, suggest Aesthetic actions somehow related to your product or service or your company.

FOOD FOR THOUGHT

One alternative approach to creating followers is a model based on mystery, wonder, and authority, often used in various fields, from politics and religion to interpersonal relationships, for manipulating people. These three elements have a deep psychological impact on people, prompting them to act or think in certain ways. Let's examine each of them in more detail.

- **Mystery**

Mystery has a powerful attraction. People, by nature, are curious and seek to uncover the unknown. When something is shrouded in mystery, it triggers interest and the desire to understand its essence. Politicians and marketers often use mystery to capture attention and maintain it. For example, secret negotiations, classified documents, or exclusive information can create a sense of belonging to something important and special. This feeling of exclusivity can be used to manipulate thoughts and actions, guiding people in the desired direction.

- **Miracle**

A miracle is an event or phenomenon that goes beyond ordinary experience and evokes feelings of amazement and wonder. The use of miracles in manipulation is based on people's tendency to believe in something extraordinary and supernatural. Religious and spiritual leaders, as well as some marketers, often use stories of miracles to strengthen their power and influence. When people believe that something is a miracle, they tend to perceive information less critically and trust more the one presenting the miracle. This allows manipulation of their thoughts and behavior, creating an illusion of power and control.

- **Authority**

Authority is the recognition or trust that a person or organization gains based on their experience, knowledge, or status. People tend to follow the instructions of those they consider authoritative figures, even if it contradicts their own beliefs. Authority can be used for manipulation by creating the image of an expert or leader whose opinion seems unquestionable. For example, advertisements often use doctors or scientists to persuade consumers of a product's effectiveness. Political leaders use authority to generate support for their decisions and actions.

These three elements—mystery, wonder, and authority—are often used in combination to enhance manipulative influence. For example, religious cults may use mystery in their rituals, tell stories of miracles, and give their leaders absolute authority. In politics, there may be classified documents (mystery), promises of "magical" solutions to problems (miracle), and undeniable leaders (authority).

The use of these elements in manipulation has ethical and moral implications. It can lead to abuse and the suppression of free will and critical thinking in people. Awareness of how these elements affect our perception and behavior can help protect ourselves from manipulation and make more conscious decisions.

Reflective task:

Taking into account the information received, describe the elements of the experience economy in your project. Conduct a review of how they are currently presented and functioning in our project.

Key conclusions of the section The Third Leg of The Tabouret Principle: the Followers

The third leg of The Tabouret Principle represents the Followers, who can be loosely divided into three groups:

- **Guests** — those who are usually content with fulfilling basic needs.

- **Regulars** — those who learn about the Unique Selling Points or Sustainable Competitive Advantage and consciously choose certain products or services going forward.

- **Advocate-Followers** — those who have been impressed and feel an emotional connection to the product or service, and as a result, take the initiative to spread the culture of using that particular product or service.

Reflective task:

Review the materials in the section "Third Leg of the Tabouret: Followers"

Mark the places (underline, highlight, make margin notes, etc.) that you think should be shared with your team. Plan where and how you will do this.

Based on your understanding of the current state of the project, assess the presence of the "Third Leg of the Tabouret" within your project.

Invite the responsible staff and agree on goals, then develop an implementation plan together.

The Seat of the Tabouret: Mission, Vision, Values

We have discussed the three legs of the Tabouret. However, a Tabouret without a seat doesn't quite look like a tabouret and looks like a bunch of sticks! Just imagine children given sticks in their hands. Especially with boys, the first thing they will do is imitate a sword fight. In business and social projects, I have sometimes seen employees from different departments or partners "competing" with each other in terms of strength or importance, trying to prove who is more significant and, consequently, whose decisions should be considered or who should make concessions. Unfortunately, this often leads to losses or even bankruptcy.

For a Tabouret to become a tabouret, a seat is necessary! There needs to be something that will unite the legs, give meaning, and bring completion to the structure! And this **Seat** is: **MISSION, VISION, VALUES**.

> *In the beginning God created the heaven and the earth. And the earth was without form, and void; and darkness was upon the face of the deep. And the Spirit of God moved upon the face of the waters. And God said, Let there be light: and there was light. And God saw the light, that it was good: and God divided the light from the darkness.*
> — *Genesis 1:1-4*

· Alex Marchuk ·

Reading about the creation of the world, one cannot help but marvel at how wonderfully everything is arranged! Our loving Creator thought of everything down to the smallest detail! Every element, from the scale of galaxies to the level of atoms, has meaning and plays its part! Each day of creation is marked by God expressing His satisfaction with the words: "It is good!" In my view, this shows that everything appeared just as our Heavenly Father intended!

> And God said, Let us make man in our image, after our likeness: and let them have dominion over the fish of the sea, and over the fowl of the air, and over the cattle, and over all the earth, and over every creeping thing that creepeth upon the earth. So God created man in his own image, in the image of God created he him; male and female created he them. And God blessed them, and God said unto them, Be fruitful, and multiply, and replenish the earth, and subdue it: and have dominion over the fish of the sea, and over the fowl of the air, and over every living thing that moveth upon the earth. And God said, Behold, I have given you every herb bearing seed, which is upon the face of all the earth, and every tree, in the which is the fruit of a tree yielding seed; to you it shall be for meat. And to every beast of the earth, and to every fowl of the air, and to every thing that creepeth upon the earth, wherein there is life, I have given every green herb for meat: and it was so. And God saw every thing that he had made, and, behold, it was very good. And the evening and the morning were the sixth day.
> — Genesis 1:26-31

Then God created man in His own image and endowed each one with free will! When God created man, He had a certain purpose in mind: "to work and take care of the earth." When humanity was created, the Lord said, "Very good!" The word translated as "very" has other meanings as well: greatly, exceedingly, immeasurably, and very. Reflecting on what God must have felt at that moment, I remember the emotions that overwhelmed me when I first saw and then held my son in my arms! When God walked with man in the Garden of Eden, when they named the animals together... The idyllic process of creation and the relationship between man and the Lord were shattered when man broke the commandment. I won't recount the Bible here, but what followed brought much sorrow to our Heavenly Father. Sometimes, perhaps even too much...

Viktor Frankl, the renowned Austrian psychologist and founder of Logotherapy, once paraphrased Nietzsche's phrase: "He who has a why to live can bear almost any how." I am almost certain that if you look back on your past and reflect on situations connected to your failures or setbacks, you will recognize that the real cause of most of them was that you didn't care much about the outcome. You didn't have an answer to the question: "Why?" As a result, when facing difficulties, you lack the strength and motivation to overcome them, and you gave up, letting things go astray.

However, the Lord does not give up, does not despair, and does not fall into hopelessness! This leads me to ask: What is it that our Heavenly Father has as His "why," which gives Him the strength to endure all our sins? And this "why" is none other than His MISSION! So, what is the mission of our Creator?

> *And Moses said unto God, Behold, when I come unto the children of Israel, and shall say unto them, The God of your fathers hath sent me unto you; and they shall say to me, What is his name? what shall I say unto them? And God said unto Moses, I AM THAT I AM: and he said, Thus shalt thou say unto the children of Israel, I AM hath sent me unto you.*
> *— Exodus 3:13-14*

"I Am Who I Am"… "The Eternal"… These are just a few of the names of God found in the Bible, but they reflect His essence! God is the Creator! The question of why God created the heavens and the earth is fundamental and deep, sparking interest both in believers and non-believers. One of the main answers to the question "Why did God create the heavens and the earth?" lies in the very nature of God as the Creator. In the Bible, God is often described as Creative and Omnipotent. His creative essence is manifested in the creation of the universe and all living things. Another important reason for creation is God's desire to reveal His Glory. The Bible tells us that the purpose of all creation is to glorify God.

> *The heavens are thine, the earth also is thine: as for the world and the fulness thereof, thou hast founded them. The north and the south thou hast created them: Tabor and Hermon shall rejoice in thy name. Thou hast a mighty arm: strong is thy hand, and high is thy right hand. Justice and judgment are the habitation of thy throne: mercy and truth shall go before thy face.*
> *— Psalm 89:11-14*

> *Let every thing that hath breath praise the LORD. Praise ye the LORD.*
> *— Psalm 150:6*

· Alex Marchuk ·

God created the world as a place where life would be sustained and flourish, where living beings could find food, water, and conditions for life. This reflects God's care and love for His creation, a desire for the support and prosperity of life. These "whys" are the reasons why our Almighty Creator does not give up, does not fall into despair, and does not abandon everything to solitude!

Just as the Lord has His own "whys," every project must have its own! Without this, sooner or later, you may find that neither you, nor your partners or colleagues, will be inspired by what you're doing. The result can be that even the smallest difficulties or misunderstandings could lead to decisions that cause either significant losses or the complete cessation of the project.

Mission is impossible without a VISION. If the Mission answers the question "why," then the Vision answers the question "where." Vision is connected with perspective, with what is yet to come, what lies beyond the present moment and the circumstances surrounding you. I call this perspective — "the best future in Jesus Christ!" Even when humanity sinned, our Creator had a vision that His creation would be with Him and that the obstacle of sin in the relationship with humans would be removed, restoring communication with them!

Behold, the days come, saith the LORD, that I will make a new covenant with the house of Israel, and with the house of Judah: Not according to the covenant that I made with their fathers in the day that I took them by the hand to bring them out of the land of Egypt; which my covenant they brake, although I was an husband unto them, saith the LORD: But this shall be the covenant that I will make with the house of Israel; After those days, saith the LORD, I will put my law in their inward parts, and write it in their hearts; and will be their God, and they shall be my people. And they shall teach no more every man his neighbour, and every man his brother, saying, Know the LORD: for they shall all know me, from the least of them unto the greatest of them, saith the LORD; for I will forgive their iniquity, and I will remember their sin no more.
— Jeremiah 31:31-34

In the beginning was the Word, and the Word was with God, and the Word was God. The same was in the beginning with God. All things were made by him; and without him was not any thing made that was made. In him was life; and the life was the light of men.

That was the true Light, which lighteth every man that cometh into the world. He was in the world, and the world was made by him, and the world knew him not. He came unto his own, and his own received him not. But as many as received him, to them gave he power to become the sons of God, even to them that believe on his name: Which were born, not of blood, nor of the will of the flesh, nor of the will of man, but of God. And the Word was made flesh, and dwelt among us, (and we beheld his glory, the glory as of the only begotten of the Father,) full of grace and truth.
— John 1:1-14

Thanks to Jesus accepting the punishment for the sins of the entire world, each of us receives justification by faith, the gift of righteousness, and the restoration of our relationship with the Heavenly Father! Even before the foundation of the universe and all that was created on Earth, God had a vision that even if man sinned, He would be able to restore the relationship with him! Praise be to the Almighty that we live in a time when any person — regardless of gender, race, age, place of residence, origin, or past doings — can take advantage of the privilege of Sonship! And this vision was with the Heavenly Father from the very beginning! The Almighty saw the mission of the Son as perfect, and through this, He saw the restoration of the relationship with His creation!

Drawing parallels with projects, it is important for each project to have a vision for its development over 1, 3, 5, or even more years. It is clear that there are many factors that influence development prospects, especially now in the context of the war in Ukraine. It is also clear that new factors may arise over time that you may not even foresee today! However, the picture of the "best future in Jesus Christ" will serve as a guiding star and inspiration for you and your team!

Viktor Frankl, in one of his books, describing the times he spent at the nazi's concentration camp, said the following about this: "I remember one morning I was walking from the camp to work, feeling that I could no longer endure the hunger, cold, and pain in my frostbitten and festering feet, which had swollen from hunger and were shoved into open shoes because of it. My situation seemed hopeless and despairing. Then I imagined that I was standing at the lectern in a large, beautiful, warm, and bright conference hall, preparing to give a lecture to an interested audience titled 'Psychotherapy in a Concentration Camp,' where I would describe exactly what I was going through at that moment. Through this technique, I somehow managed to rise above the situation, above the present, and above the suffering, and see it as if it were already in the past, and I, with all my suffering, became an object of scientific psychological research, which I myself was conducting."

If you have a vision of the "best future in Jesus Christ," and if you share this vision not only with your team but also with your partners and followers, you will be able to receive support, resources, and perhaps your vision will become an example and inspiration for someone else!

The last point of the Seat is VALUES. After Adam broke the one commandment related to the fruit of the "tree of knowledge of good and evil," shame and fear entered human life.

> *And the eyes of them both were opened, and they knew that they were naked; and they sewed fig leaves together, and made themselves aprons. And they heard the voice of the LORD God walking in the garden in the cool of the day: and Adam and his wife hid themselves from the presence of the LORD God amongst the trees of the garden. And the LORD God called unto Adam, and said unto him, Where art thou? And he said, I heard thy voice in the garden, and I was afraid, because I was naked; and I hid myself.*
> — *Genesis 3:7-10*

And with the next generation, envy and violence entered the lives of people.

> *And in process of time it came to pass, that Cain brought of the fruit of the ground an offering unto the LORD. And Abel, he also brought of the firstlings of his flock and of the fat thereof. And the LORD had respect unto Abel and to his offering: But unto Cain and to his offering he had not respect. And Cain was very wroth, and his countenance fell.*
> — *Genesis 4:3-5*

> *And Cain talked with Abel his brother: and it came to pass, when they were in the field, that Cain rose up against Abel his brother, and slew him.*
> — *Genesis 4:8*

What happened next shows that some people seemed to intentionally seek various ways to explore the depths of turning away from the Lord!

For the invisible things of him from the creation of the world are clearly seen, being understood by the things that are made, even his eternal power and Godhead; so that they are without excuse: Because that, when they knew God, they glorified him not as God, neither were thankful; but became vain in their imaginations, and their foolish heart was darkened. Professing themselves to be wise, they became fools, And changed the glory of the uncorruptible God into an image made like to corruptible man, and to birds, and fourfooted beasts, and creeping things. Wherefore God also gave them up to uncleanness through the lusts of their own hearts, to dishonour their own bodies between themselves: Who changed the truth of God into a lie, and worshipped and served the creature more than the Creator, who is blessed for ever. Amen. For this cause God gave them up unto vile affections: for even their women did change the natural use into that which is against nature: And likewise also the men, leaving the natural use of the woman, burned in their lust one toward another; men with men working that which is unseemly, and receiving in themselves that recompence of their error which was meet. And even as they did not like to retain God in their knowledge, God gave them over to a reprobate mind, to do those things which are not convenient; Being filled with all unrighteousness, fornication, wickedness, covetousness, maliciousness; full of envy, murder, debate, deceit, malignity; whisperers, Backbiters, haters of God, despiteful, proud, boasters, inventors of evil things, disobedient to parents, Without understanding, covenantbreakers, without natural affection, implacable, unmerciful: Who knowing the judgment of God, that they which commit such things are worthy of death, not only do the same, but have pleasure in them that do them.
— Romans 1:20-32

Therefore, when the Lord brought the Israelites out of Egypt, in the wilderness, the commandments were given to the Jews, with adherence to them being linked to blessings, and failure to follow them leading to curses!

And God spake all these words, saying, I am the LORD thy God, which have brought thee out of the land of Egypt, out of the house of bondage. Thou shalt have no other gods before me. Thou shalt

not make unto thee any graven image, or any likeness of any thing that is in heaven above, or that is in the earth beneath, or that is in the water under the earth: Thou shalt not bow down thyself to them, nor serve them: for I the LORD thy God am a jealous God, visiting the iniquity of the fathers upon the children unto the third and fourth generation of them that hate me; And shewing mercy unto thousands of them that love me, and keep my commandments. Thou shalt not take the name of the LORD thy God in vain; for the LORD will not hold him guiltless that taketh his name in vain. Remember the sabbath day, to keep it holy. Six days shalt thou labour, and do all thy work: But the seventh day is the sabbath of the LORD thy God: in it thou shalt not do any work, thou, nor thy son, nor thy daughter, thy manservant, nor thy maidservant, nor thy cattle, nor thy stranger that is within thy gates: For in six days the LORD made heaven and earth, the sea, and all that in them is, and rested the seventh day: wherefore the LORD blessed the sabbath day, and hallowed it. Honour thy father and thy mother: that thy days may be long upon the land which the LORD thy God giveth thee. Thou shalt not kill. Thou shalt not commit adultery. Thou shalt not steal. Thou shalt not bear false witness against thy neighbour. Thou shalt not covet thy neighbour's house, thou shalt not covet thy neighbour's wife, nor his manservant, nor his maidservant, nor his ox, nor his ass, nor any thing that is thy neighbour's.
— Exodus 20:1-17

These commandments became a pivotal moment in the history of the Israelites and played a huge role in shaping their understanding of good and evil, justice, and mercy. On one hand, receiving the commandments solidified the special relationship between the Israelites and God, affirming the closeness of Israel and giving a sense of uniqueness and responsibility before God. On the other hand, the commandments played a decisive role in shaping the legal system and societal order. The Ten Commandments, like other laws in the Pentateuch, provided the Israelites with a detailed code of norms and rules that governed all aspects of their lives, creating a society where justice, equality, and social fairness became fundamental principles. These laws helped maintain order and harmony, ensuring the stability and security of the community. The shared acceptance of God's laws promoted unity among the people, transforming them into one nation with common values and goals. This sense of community helped the Israelites overcome difficulties and trials, strengthening them in their fight for survival and prosperity.

A famous character from Ilf and Petrov's work "The Golden Calf," Ostap Bender, knew "four hundred relatively honest ways of taking money from people." When there is a task or goal, there are usually at least several ways to accomplish it or achieve it. Some of them may involve violating certain moral-ethical norms, while others may even break the law and lead to administrative or criminal prosecution! Which of these methods are acceptable to you? Are you willing to tolerate certain violations if the goal is achieved?

In addition to tasks and goals, there are also relationships within the team and with the target audience, as well as attitudes towards one's duties and the organization's property. These areas can also vary! Conflicts, gossip, rudeness, negligence, irresponsibility... Unfortunately, sometimes one has to deal with various behavioral manifestations of team members, both towards each other and towards the target audience and partners. What are you willing to tolerate, and what are you not?

These questions, among others, are meant to regulate Values. Of course, there are state laws, and if a team member violates them, they will be held responsible and punished. However, in addition to state laws, there is also an internal code — values that each team member is expected to adhere to if they are interested in working within this team!

Next, we will explore MISSION, VISION, and VALUES in more detail.

The Seat of the Tabouret Principle: the Mission

Mission (from Latin, act of sending, from mittere to send) — a specific task with which a person or a group is charged; a preestablished and often self-imposed objective or purpose; a strong inner impulse toward a particular course of action, especially when accompanied by conviction of divine influence.

If you can confidently answer "yes" to the statements below, it means that this component of successful work is, to some extent, implemented in your project:

- You have a clearly defined mission statement that is shared by all team members, indicating the purpose, field of activity, and a specific target audience.

For my name's sake will I defer mine anger, and for my praise will
I refrain for thee, that I cut thee not off. Behold, I have refined thee,
but not with silver; I have chosen thee in the furnace of affliction. For
mine own sake, even for mine own sake, will I do it: for how should
my name be polluted? and I will not give my glory unto another.
— *Isaiah 48:9-11*

From Adam onward, people have repeatedly deviated from the Lord's commandments. Even the prophets and patriarchs, who are mentioned in the Scriptures and are role models for each of us, also made mistakes and made decisions that went against the will of the Creator. For example, Abraham, who is called "the friend of God," took his nephew Lot with him, when the Lord told him to take only his family; introduced his wife Sarah as his sister, fearing that he would be killed because of her beauty; and had a son, Ishmael, by a concubine. Nevertheless, the Lord, being "longsuffering and gracious," showed mercy, gave everyone a chance to realize their mistakes and turn around. There is something more for which the Lord shows mercy and blesses people! This "more" is a connecting line throughout the Bible, and it is connected to God Himself and His essence:

And the LORD descended in the cloud, and stood with him there,
and proclaimed the name of the LORD. And the LORD passed by
before him, and proclaimed, The LORD, The LORD God, merciful
and gracious, longsuffering, and abundant in goodness and truth,
Keeping mercy for thousands, forgiving iniquity and transgression
and sin, and that will by no means clear the guilty; visiting the
iniquity of the fathers upon the children, and upon the children's
children, unto the third and to the fourth generation.
— *Exodus 34:5-7*

When we look at the "heroes of faith," we must admit that each of them had difficulties and trials on their life path. However, something more inspired them not to give up halfway through, but to go on to the end. Each of the heroes of faith had their own "whys". And this "for the sake of why" gave them the strength to overcome difficulties, to remain faithful to God when people around them turned away from the Lord and His commandments! Let's look at what the Bible says about this:

ABRAHAM:

We have already mentioned the circumstances and challenges that Abraham faced. He left his homeland and became a stranger, experienced crop failures, faced threats to his life while in Egypt and the land of the Philistines, fought bravely to win back his nephew... One of the greatest challenges was that God's promise of a descendant from Sarah had not been fulfilled for 25 years! And what a challenge from the Lord to sacrifice his favorite son, Isaac! You must admit that you need to have a very good reason "why" to go through these challenges and remain faithful! I believe that God's promises to Abraham were just that "why":

Seeing that Abraham shall surely become a great and mighty nation, and all the nations of the earth shall be blessed in him? For I know him, that he will command his children and his household after him, and they shall keep the way of the LORD, to do justice and judgment; that the LORD may bring upon Abraham that which he hath spoken of him.
— Genesis 18:18-19

ISAAC:

The fate of Isaac was in some ways similar to that of his father Abraham. He was also a stranger, he also faced threats to his life, crop failures, and his wife Rebekah could not get pregnant for a long time... Despite this, he remained faithful to God and managed to pass on his faith to his children. When one of his sons, Jacob, was far away from his father's house, he prayed to the Lord and addressed Him as follows: "God of my father Abraham, and God of my father Isaac." That is, in this way, he acknowledged that his father Isaac had worshipped the Lord! So, Isaac also had his own "why":

And God said, Sarah thy wife shall bear thee a son indeed; and thou shalt call his name Isaac: and I will establish my covenant with him for an everlasting covenant, and with his seed after him. And as for Ishmael, I have heard thee: Behold, I have blessed him, and will make him fruitful, and will multiply him exceedingly; twelve princes shall he beget, and I will make him a great nation. But my covenant will I establish with Isaac, which Sarah shall bear unto thee at this set time in the next year.
— Exodus 17:19-21

JACOB:

Jacob first had to flee from his home because his brother Esau threatened to take revenge for the stolen blessing, and then he had to flee from his father-in-law Laban because he wanted to take his property... The death of his beloved wife, the loss of his son Joseph, whom he thought had been torn apart by wild animals, crop failures — there were many trials, but Jacob had his "whys" that allowed him to remain faithful:

> And Jacob went out from Beer-sheba, and went toward Haran. And he lighted upon a certain place, and tarried there all night, because the sun was set; and he took of the stones of that place, and put them for his pillows, and lay down in that place to sleep. And he dreamed, and behold a ladder set up on the earth, and the top of it reached to heaven: and behold the angels of God ascending and descending on it. And, behold, the LORD stood above it, and said, I am the LORD God of Abraham thy father, and the God of Isaac: the land whereon thou liest, to thee will I give it, and to thy seed; And thy seed shall be as the dust of the earth, and thou shalt spread abroad to the west, and to the east, and to the north, and to the south: and in thee and in thy seed shall all the families of the earth be blessed. And, behold, I am with thee, and will keep thee in all places whither thou goest, and will bring thee again into this land; for I will not leave thee, until I have done that which I have spoken to thee of.
> — Genesis 28:10-15

Whichever of the leaders of the Old Testament you look at, each of them faced extraordinary challenges, but they also had a strong "why" that prevailed and inspired them to go on to the end! Moses, Samuel, and David — each of the biblical heroes went through a series of trials because they sincerely had convictions and believed in their "why."

And what about the New Testament? How are things there?

APOSTLE PETER:

One of the greatest trials for Peter was the arrest of Jesus Christ. His cowardice led him to deny the Lord three times! But later on, Peter became one of the most authoritative preachers and the head of the church, who not only went through prison and torture, but also died as a martyr in Rome. Peter had his own "why", which for a moment was overshadowed by fear for his life, but later he recovered and finished his work!

He saith unto them, But whom say ye that I am? And Simon Peter answered and said, Thou art the Christ, the Son of the living God. And Jesus answered and said unto him, Blessed art thou, Simon Barjona: for flesh and blood hath not revealed it unto thee, but my Father which is in heaven. And I say also unto thee, That thou art Peter, and upon this rock I will build my church; and the gates of hell shall not prevail against it. And I will give unto thee the keys of the kingdom of heaven: and whatsoever thou shalt bind on earth shall be bound in heaven: and whatsoever thou shalt loose on earth shall be loosed in heaven.
— Matthew 16:15-19

APOSTLE PAUL:

Apostle Paul is well known not only for his letters, which are an integral part of the New Testament, but also for being present at the stoning of Stephen and guarding the clothes of those who stoned him. Let's look at what he himself says about his trials:

Are they ministers of Christ? (I speak as a fool) I am more; in labours more abundant, in stripes above measure, in prisons more frequent, in deaths oft. Of the Jews five times received I forty stripes save one. Thrice was I beaten with rods, once was I stoned, thrice I suffered shipwreck, a night and a day I have been in the deep; In journeyings often, in perils of waters, in perils of robbers, in perils by mine own countrymen, in perils by the heathen, in perils in the city, in perils in the wilderness, in perils in the sea, in perils among false brethren; In weariness and painfulness, in watchings often, in hunger and thirst, in fastings often, in cold and nakedness. Beside those things that are without, that which cometh upon me daily, the care of all the churches.
— 2 Corinthians 11:23-28

What was it about Paul that allowed him to overcome all the circumstances and eventually accept martyrdom with dignity? As you may have guessed, Paul had his own "why".

> *And this I do for the gospel's sake, that I might be partaker thereof with you. Know ye not that they which run in a race run all, but one receiveth the prize? So run, that ye may obtain. And every man that striveth for the mastery is temperate in all things. Now they do it to obtain a corruptible crown; but we an incorruptible. I therefore so run, not as uncertainly; so fight I, not as one that beateth the air: But I keep under my body, and bring it into subjection: lest that by any means, when I have preached to others, I myself should be a castaway.*
> — *1 Corinthians 9:23-27*

Each of these heroes faced circumstances that could have served as an excuse to give up and "live like everyone else." But thanks to them, today we have examples worthy of emulation that inspire us to go on despite the obstacles.

Just imagine what results you can achieve if you and each of your team members know what you are doing for and it truly inspires you! Any project should have the highest goal, which will be related to what makes my yard, neighborhood, city, region, country, and the world a better place! The mission is one of those elements that unite people into a team and gives them the ability to come to an agreement, move as one, supporting and helping each other. Sometimes this requires putting aside your ambitions and compromising... It's not just a formal declaration, it's the heart and soul of the company, which guides its actions and inspires employees to achieve high goals. And this is possible only when a person understands the answer to this question: "Why?" or "Why do I need this?

FOOD FOR THOUGHT

At the beginning of my leadership career, I faced one of the challenges that helped me overcome the understanding of the mission.

It was around 1996-1997. Working for a company that produced and sold chocolates and coffee, we faced a situation where a number of importers were selling their products much cheaper due to the fact that they did not pay taxes on imports. However, thanks to marketing, our products were in demand and had some of the highest sales figures. One of the elements that allowed us to achieve this was a rather aggressive policy of placing goods in stores — as a rule, we made sure that our products were placed in the best places where they could be easily seen by customers. And then one day, several members of my team raised the issue that other manufacturers also want to sell their products and therefore they cannot be "cheeky" and occupy these places only with our products. This question puzzled me, because I tried to be a leader who does not just set some unattainable goals and who cares how the goals are achieved. On the contrary, I have always clearly understood what needs to be done and how to achieve the goals set for the team. I shared this with the head of our company. He replied that, unlike other suppliers who avoid paying taxes, our company pays all taxes, fills the pension fund, creates jobs in Ukraine, not only within our company but also in related areas (ingredients, packaging, logistics), attracts foreign investment to the country...

This conversation inspired me so much that I was able to pass this inspiration on to my team and as a result, our products continued to take the best places on the shelves!

Unfortunately, sometimes company owners and managers take a formal approach to mission statements. I have met companies that had a mission, but it did not fulfill its tasks! If the mission is formulated as a slogan, as a sign for the outside world, then, as a rule, it inspires few team members and does not cause the positive effect that it is potentially intended to perform!

For a mission statement not to be an empty formality, but to truly inspire everyone, it must answer three key questions:

1. FOR WHOM?

The first and most important aspect of the mission is the recipient of our activities. These are the people for whom the organization exists and whose needs it seeks to meet. Defining a clear addressee helps each employee understand who they are working for and whose interests they are protecting. This can be your target audience or clients, patients, students, residents of a particular region, or the general public.

When employees realize that their work directly affects the well-being of specific individuals or groups, it improves discipline and increases their sense of responsibility and significance.

2. HOW?

The next important component of the mission is a description of how the organization achieves its goals, i.e. the scope of its activities. This includes the methods, principles and approaches used to get the job done. A clear and honest statement of the areas of activity helps employees understand how they can contribute to the overall goal.

An effective mission statement should reflect the unique characteristics and values of the organization. For example, if a company is focused on innovation, its mission statement can emphasize the desire for continuous improvement and the adoption of advanced technologies. This will inspire employees to work creatively and find new solutions.

3. WHAT IS THE BIGGER PICTURE?

The last but not least aspect is what the organization exists for. This is the philosophical and ideological component of the mission that goes beyond the immediate goals and objectives. It answers the question: "Why are we doing this? What is the highest purpose we serve?"

When an organization's mission is focused on more than just profit, it can inspire a deep sense of engagement and belonging among employees. For example, if the mission of an environmental organization is to preserve the planet for future generations, it encourages employees to work with enthusiasm and dedication, knowing that they are making the world a better place.

Thus, for an organization's mission to be inspirational rather than formal, it must clearly answer three key questions: who the organization works for, how it achieves its goals, and what is the larger purpose for which it exists. The target audience helps employees understand whom they serve and whom they help. A description of the areas of activity and methods of work gives a clear picture of how employees can contribute. And the ideological component of the mission, focused on a higher purpose, creates a deep sense of involvement and commitment, motivating each employee to work with enthusiasm and purpose.

· Alex Marchuk ·

When an organization's mission meets these criteria, it becomes a powerful source of inspiration that unites all employees around a common goal and encourages them to achieve outstanding results. One of the key factors that brings a company's mission to life is the example of the company's founders and leaders. If people see that the leaders sincerely believe and share what they declare, then they will be inspired. If they see falsity and indifference, the mission will most likely not inspire them either.

Here are a few examples of missions from companies I've worked with that help us understand their missions:

Mondelez International — One of the world leaders in the production and sale of food products (snacks).

Mission: Every day, we work to shape the future of snacking around the world by offering consumers the right snacks, at the right time, and made right. With our wide range of snacks, consumers can choose what they need, when they need it. Any product is more satisfying when you know it's made with high-quality ingredients and without harming the planet. From our dedicated chocolatiers and bakers around the world to the snacking moment, at Mondelēz International we know how to inspire people to snack right.

Colgate Palmolive — One of the world's leaders in oral and body care.

Mission: We are Colgate — a caring, innovative, fast-growing company that offers a new vision of a healthier future for all people, their pets and our planet.

Philips — One of the world's leaders in the production and sale of electronics and medical equipment.

Mission: At Philips, our goal is to improve people's health and well-being through meaningful innovation. As a technology company, we and our brand licensees innovate for people with a single conviction: there is always a way to make life better.

Fit Curves — An international franchise of fitness centers for women. The founders of the company have developed a special training and nutrition program that helps women to be healthy and happy by developing a conscious habit of training, eating right and unleashing their personal potential.

Mission: We help our clients to gain the power to be healthy and happy by developing a conscious habit of training, eating right and unleashing their personal potential. We are creating a community of healthy and happy women who bring a healthy lifestyle to their loved ones.

Health Island — The company operated a network of centers selling massage equipment.

Mission: Serving the nation by serving the individual. Every day, we care about the health of the nation through the personal service of Health Island consultants to their clients and visitors.

Expert Food Service — One of the regional leaders in the production and sale of coffee.

Mission: We promote coffee culture so that every coffee connoisseur in every city can enjoy the aroma and taste of the best coffee, and coffee shop owners can maximize their benefits!

Tabouret Advisory Agency — A team of professionals who advise, counsel, and support businesses and ministries using biblical principles as a foundation.

Mission: Through the implementation of the Tabouret principle in businesses and ministries, we help to increase their efficiency and positive impact on the world around them!

These missions are aimed at improving people's lives, creating innovative products and services, and making a positive impact on society and the environment. They help guide companies in their actions, inspiring employees and customers to achieve common goals and high results.

FOOD FOR THOUGHT

Make the mission statement one of the key questions in your job interviews. See how the candidate responds to it. If the mission of your organization resonates with him, you will most likely find a loyal and responsible team member who will treat the organization and the team like a family. If it doesn't mean much to him, then he will most likely be more focused on remuneration and career growth.

Reflective task:

Does your project have a mission statement? Based on the information above, invite key employees and revise the mission statement together so that it truly inspires each team member.

The Seat of the Tabouret: Vision

Vision (for the Organization) – the act or power of seeingце; something seen in a dream, trance, or ecstasy; a thought, concept, or object formed by the imagination; the act or power of imagination; something seen.

I also call vision as "better future in Jesus Christ".

If you can confidently answer "yes" to the statements below, it means that this component of successful work is, to some extent, implemented in your project:

- You have an agreed upon and written picture of the project's development - Vision - for the period of 1-3-5-10 years or more

- You have a properly defined goal for the year, quarter, month...

- You have agreed and documented strategies and plans that will help you realize your Vision and achieve your goals

*And I saw a new heaven and a new earth: for the first heaven and
the first earth were passed away; and there was no more sea. And I
John saw the holy city, new Jerusalem, coming down from God out
of heaven, prepared as a bride adorned for her husband. And I heard
a great voice out of heaven saying, Behold, the tabernacle of God is
with men, and he will dwell with them, and they shall be his people,
and God himself shall be with them, and be their God.*
— Revelation 21:1-3

The Word of God says that in Heaven, Our Lord is surrounded by angels who
keep repeating: "Holy! Holy! Holy!" In another place, it is said that the foundation
of the throne of our Lord is righteousness! Sin and impurity can have nothing
to do with our Creator. When the first man sinned and was expelled from the
Garden of Eden, the Lord still had a VISION of a future where people would
still be with Him!

A vision, which is usually more general, is supported by a more specific PURPOSE.
The Lord has a PURPOSE because He wants to be with His creation, that is, with
us! To make this possible, it was necessary to remove the barrier between us
and the Lord! This barrier was sin. In other words, in order to realize the Vision,
the Lord had to somehow achieve the Goal of removing sin from His creation!

**Purpose or Goal — something set up as an object or end to be
attained; a subject under discussion or an action in the course of
execution.**

Our heavenly Father also has a STRATEGY. Given the holiness of our Creator
and the fact that nothing unclean can be in His presence, He had a Strategy to
make sinful people sinless! How did He do it? Through blood. This was the case
with the first man — the Lord clothed Adam and Eve in the skin of animals that
had been sacrificed. It was the same hundreds of years later, when the Israelites
sacrificed their own animals to symbolize the process of redemption.

**Strategy — a careful plan or method; an adaptation or complex of
adaptations (as of behavior, metabolism, or structure) that serves
or appears to serve an important function in achieving evolutionary
success.**

But the blood of animals does not remove the sin and guilt that separates the
Lord and His creation forever! It had to be done again and again! And God
had a plan to bring salvation from guilt and sin once and for all to millions of

people — through the sacrifice of His only begotten Son — who would believe in Jesus Christ and receive Him as their Lord and Savior! By accepting Jesus and believing in Him, everyone receives the amazing gift of being a beloved child of God! In other words, everyone has a future, a future! And even if someone is in a dead end, in darkness, has done some bad things, there is still hope for such a person, there is a future!

Plan — a drawing or diagram drawn; a method for achieving an end; an orderly arrangement of parts of an overall design or objective.

This is what the **VISION** is responsible for: **PURPOSE, STRATEGY,** and **PLAN,** which are closely interconnected! Vision is another important element that unites people around a project. Vision is the compass of an organization that points the way to the future and unites all participants on the path to common goals. It not only sets the direction but also inspires employees, customers, and partners, encouraging them to strive for greatness. It should be ambitious but realistic and set specific goals for the coming years. This helps employees understand what they want and work in unison to achieve a common goal. The vision should show how the organization's success will impact the lives of employees and society as a whole. When people realize that their work is making a difference, it increases their motivation and commitment. For a vision to fully fulfill its role, it must answer the following questions:

- Where are we going as a project (organization)?

- What will happen and where will we be in three, five… or more years?

- How will my life, family, loved ones, house, neighborhood, city, country, world change if we are successful in what we do?

You have to admit that any person who has a vision will act with more consciousness and be more motivated than a person who has no idea of the future and acts based on the current moment. Obviously, if you have an idea of where you want to be in a few years, it will be much easier for you to set your priorities. Knowing your priorities, you will be able to plan your time and efforts much more efficiently, because you can assess how much this or that activity brings you closer or not closer to your Vision. Consequently, you will spend less time and effort on things that do not bring you closer to your Vision and, on the contrary, focus more on things that make you closer to your Vision! At the personal level, you will be able to regulate the problem of "hanging out in social networks" or "killing time" much easier! You have an alternative — some actions that help you move forward!

FOOD FOR THOUGHT

Imagination is more important than knowledge. Knowledge is limited. Imagination surrounds the world. - Albert Einstein

Reflective task:

Does your project have a vision for 3, 5, or more years? Based on the above information, try dreaming on your own or invite key employees and revise the vision together to include a "better future" for each team member.

Unlike the Vision, which is usually formulated as a general picture or image of the future, without specific fixation on terms and quantitative indicators, the PURPOSE or GOAL has specific criteria that, thanks to the first leg of the Tabouret (System), allow for a clear assessment of its achievement. That is why the SMART approach is used to set goals, which helps to formulate clear and achievable goals. The word "smart" itself has meaning as: having or showing a high degree of mental ability... But it also has the additional meaning! The decoding of the SMART abbreviation is as follows:

- **Specific:** The goal should be clear, understandable, and specifically defined. Avoid generalizations and state exactly what you want to achieve. Let's use the example of a coffee shop: Instead of "Increase sales," say "Increase the number of servings of coffee with milk and/or desserts sold."

- **Measurable**: The result must be expressed in quantifiable terms so that progress can be evaluated. Example: Instead of "Increase sales" again, say "Increase sales of coffee with milk by 20%."

- **Achievable:** The goal should be realistic and take into account the resources available (time, budget, team). Example: Instead of "Double sales in one week," state "Increase sales of coffee with milk by 20% in one month."

- **Relevant:** The goal should be in line with your priorities and important to the business or project. Example: Instead of "Add sushi to the coffee shop menu," say "Add three new desserts to the coffee shop menu that go well with coffee."

- **Time-bound:** You need to define a clear deadline (schedule, deadline) by which the goal must be achieved. Example: Instead of "Conduct training," say "Conduct training for employees by December 31."

Reflective task:

Based on this information, try to identify several SMART goals for a particular area of activity within your project. Invite key employees of a particular department and review the relevant goals together to ensure that they are consistent with the SMART approach.

The Vision and Goals should be supported by a solid Strategy that describes the direction the organization will take to achieve the Vision and Goals. The Strategy should include an analysis of current resources and capabilities, as well as an action plan to help the organization overcome obstacles and achieve its goals. The strategy defines how you can achieve your Vision! To demonstrate the essence of strategy, I suggest looking at athletes preparing for the Olympic Games. For example, if an athlete aims to win the 100-meter dash, their strategy will be related to the development of explosive power and speed. In contrast, an athlete who aims to win a marathon will develop endurance and stability.

To be meaningful, the Strategy should be formulated on the basis of the following rules:

1. It must be based on a clear understanding of the mission and vision. The strategy statement must be aligned with the mission and vision to ensure long-term relevance.

2. A meaningful strategy assumes that you have analyzed your organization (internal factors) and the market (external factors). Internal factors relate to the following: marketing, operations, sales, technology, finance, team... As for external factors, they relate to the target audience, competitors, supply chain (which is directly involved in the transfer of goods/services to the target audience), and macroeconomic factors. This will allow you to assess the real situation and focus on what has the greatest potential for development. Such an analysis is also called a SWOT analysis, where:

    ·   **S — Strengths** — identifies the internal factors that are your strengths and, accordingly, which you can rely on to achieve your goals;

    ·   **W — Weaknesses** — identifies the internal factors that are your weaknesses and, accordingly, which you need to improve to be able to achieve your goals;

    ·   **O — Opportunities** — identifies external factors that open up opportunities for growth and development;

    ·   **T — Threats** — identifies external factors that, on the contrary, are associated with risks and threats to your project.

3. Based on the **SWOT** analysis, you will be able to objectively see what exactly can be your Unique Selling Points (Sustainable Competitive Advantage), which sets you apart from your competitors and makes your target audience choose you! Your strategy should essentially be built around your UCP and its use.

4. The strategy should be supported by short-term goals and clear action plans to achieve them. We have discussed the approach to goals above. In accordance with the first leg of The Tabouret Principle, your plans should be structured in such a way that at any given time, you can clearly understand what is happening with a particular goal and who is responsible for it.

Reflective task:

Based on the gathered information, try to conduct a SWOT analysis and analyze the internal and external factors, identify the USP, and formulate a well-founded strategy. The next step is to define goals and develop plans to achieve them.

Invite key employees and together review the SWOT analysis, i.e., internal and external factors, identified USP, and strategy.

The Seat of the Tabouret: Values

Value — the monetary worth of something; a fair return or equivalent in goods, services, or money for something exchanged; relative worth, utility, or importance; something (such as a principle or quality) intrinsically valuable or desirable; a numerical quantity that is assigned or is determined by calculation or measurement.

Culture (corporate) — the customary beliefs, social forms, and material traits of a racial, religious, or social group; the set of shared attitudes, values, goals, and practices that characterizes an institution or organization; the set of values, conventions, or social practices associated with a particular field, activity, or societal characteristic; the integrated pattern of human knowledge, belief, and behavior that depends upon the capacity for learning and transmitting knowledge to succeeding generations.

If you can confidently answer "yes" to the statements below, it means that this component of successful work is, to some extent, implemented in your project:

- You have a written code of conduct and/or charter for behavior within the team and with the outside world, including suppliers and clients. Moreover, this information is regularly updated.

And Moses came and called for the elders of the people, and laid before their faces all these words which the LORD commanded him. And all the people answered together, and said, All that the LORD hath spoken we will do. And Moses returned the words of the people unto the LORD.
— Exodus 19:7-8

There are about eight billion people on planet Earth, and no two are exactly the same. Each of us differs from others not only in external parameters such as gender, height, weight, appearance, or fingerprints, but also has unique personality traits, life experiences, talents... Therefore, when two or more people start interacting in some way, it is vitally important to agree on how the interaction will take place and how decisions will be made. In order to help avoid actions that could harm us or others, God gave people commandments or in other words, VALUES.

FOOD FOR THOUGHT

In any team, even if the team consists of just two people—such as a family, for example—it is important to have agreed-upon rules for interaction and decision-making. Recently, the "prenuptial agreement" has become quite popular worldwide. Couples who decide to marry create and document agreements that outline their relationship and the consequences if one party breaches these agreements. One can have different views on this practice, but it certainly gives each party the opportunity to make decisions based not only on emotions but also on common sense.

If we look at God's commandments, four out of the ten are related to the relationship between people and the Lord, and six concern relationships between people. That is why, when Jesus was asked about the most important commandment, He summarized the ten commandments into two:

Master, which is the great commandment in the law? Jesus said unto him, Thou shalt love the Lord thy God with all thy heart, and with all thy soul, and with all thy mind. This is the first and great commandment. And the second is like unto it, Thou shalt love thy neighbour as thyself. On these two commandments hang all the law and the prophets.
— Matthew 22:36-40

· Alex Marchuk ·

In other words, Jesus first emphasizes the importance of striving towards the Lord and seeking God's direction in our lives. If this is in place, then the second part — concerning our neighbor — will be filled not with selfishness and pride, but with sincere love, modeled after love for oneself. To better understand what "love" means in the divine sense, I suggest reviewing the following definition of the word "love":

> *Charity suffereth long, and is kind; charity envieth not; charity vaunteth not itself, is not puffed up, Doth not behave itself unseemly, seeketh not her own, is not easily provoked, thinketh no evil; Rejoiceth not in iniquity, but rejoiceth in the truth; Beareth all things, believeth all things, hopeth all things, endureth all things. Charity never faileth: but whether there be prophecies, they shall fail; whether there be tongues, they shall cease; whether there be knowledge, it shall vanish away.*
> *— 1 Corinthians 13:4-8*

If, in your opinion, this level of values is already sufficiently high, then look at the words of Jesus, which He said during the Last Supper:

> *A new commandment I give unto you, That ye love one another; as I have loved you, that ye also love one another. By this shall all men know that ye are my disciples, if ye have love one to another.*
> *— John 13:34-35*

Jesus invites us to raise the bar from loving our neighbor as ourselves to loving others as He has loved us! And how did Jesus love each of us? That's right, He gave His life for each of us! The Holy and Sinless One took the punishment for the unclean and sinful, thus granting us salvation and righteousness in the present and eternal life in the future!

When we talk about values, it's not the well-formulated slogans that matter the most, but the example set by leaders! The English have an interesting proverb: "Your actions speak so loudly that I can't hear your words!" From the example of the Israelite kings, we can see that when the kings were obedient to God, the enemies retreated, and there was abundance and order in the land. When the kings began to worship idols, enemies came, strife followed, and the country experienced decline.

Unfortunately, in the post-Soviet space, there is quite a blurred understanding of values, both at the individual, family, and community levels. This is largely because our society is still going through its stages of development and is in the process of forming a demand for values and dignity. Every day, we encounter situations that are glaring: even during the full-scale war of Russia against Ukraine, we witness numerous cases of corruption, irresponsibility, and lawlessness... Just imagine the level of development any country could achieve if its leaders made decisions based on the values of Jesus! History provides examples of leaders who put aside their potential gain and made decisions in the best interests of their communities and countries! One such example is Singapore — a country that, thanks to the leadership of Lee Kuan Yew, jumped from the "third world to the first" and is now one of the most developed countries in the world!

Returning to values at the level of project/organization, it is also important to understand their connection with motivators. Together, Values form what is called Corporate Culture, which regulates behavioral norms both within the team and organization, as well as externally. We have already mentioned Viktor Frankl, the famous Austrian psychotherapist and founder of logotherapy. In one of his books, he described three main types of behavior that people exhibit in response to external conditions:

1. Conformism or "to do as everyone else does"

This type of behavior occurs when a person adapts to the expectations and demands of society or their environment. They passively accept norms, values, and rules without questioning their appropriateness or morality. This behavior can lead to a loss of personal freedom and identity on one hand, and on the other hand, to apathy and irresponsibility. An employee who chooses this behavior simply formally aligns with your corporate culture. Nothing more! If you expect more, such as working overtime, putting in extra effort to achieve goals, or defending the organization's image, you're unlikely to get any of it!

2. Totalitarianism or "I'm the boss, you're the fool"

This behavior occurs when a person tries to impose their will on others by using power, coercion, or manipulation. This position implies control over employees, denying their freedom, and simultaneously absolving them of responsibility for a lack of initiative, inactivity, or irresponsibility. Why bother with initiative?! Why do more?! All that's needed is to follow orders and provide a report. It doesn't matter if there's no result. The important thing is that I've done my part!

3. Transcendence or "Conscious Dignity"

This type of behavior, according to Frankl, is the highest manifestation of human nature. A person goes beyond their own selfish interests, overcoming limitations and difficulties, to find the meaning of life. It is the ability to prioritize higher values such as love, service, or creativity over personal suffering or the desire for power. This behavior arises when an employee is "in the right place at the right time." In other words, when what they do and who they do it with resonates with their heart and truly aligns with their understanding of the meaning of life! Such employees will not only work overtime out of their own initiative, but they will also put maximum effort into achieving goals, showing concern for any issues related to the organization, and encouraging others by setting an example.

Of course, in light of the behavior types above, it is desirable for us to foster a conscious attitude within the team towards implementing the principles of Corporate Culture. To do so, we must implement all the "legs" of the Tabouret and ensure that each element works at full capacity!

FOOD FOR THOUGHT

When I worked at one of the international companies, I realized firsthand how much corporate culture can differ from one company to another. This was my second international experience. In the first company, the leader was a mature and wise individual who encouraged open discussions about work-related matters. At the weekly management meetings (Board of Management), which I attended, we openly discussed all work-related issues, did "brainstorming" sessions, and sometimes even argued and criticized each other's decisions and results! Of course, it was important not to make things personal and to follow the rule: "Be tough on the problem, soft on the person!"

In the second company, my functional manager was Turkish. Unfortunately, I realized later that he practiced an authoritarian management style. So, when I expressed and justified my opinion during a discussion about the sales strategy of the company's products in Ukraine, he became extremely outraged and subsequently reduced our communication to pure formality, never missing an opportunity to throw obstacles in my way.

One notable example was a few meetings related to the year-end review and goal-setting for the upcoming year. During the first such meeting I participated in, when I proudly presented our achievements, including a 60% increase in sales, his reaction was as follows: "It's easy to show growth when you're comparing it to 'zero'!" He implied that the results from the previous year, before I joined the company, were extremely weak in his opinion. The second year, after my presentation, he emotionally expressed that I exceeded the budget and, in general, was too independent. After this, there was an awkward pause, and one of his senior colleagues remarked: "Maybe that's true, but Ukraine has been the best division in the world for two years running!" By the second year of my work, our sales had increased by over 40% compared to the previous year!

Honestly, such behavior from my manager created a certain pressure on me. Perhaps some people would have passed that pressure onto their subordinates, venting their frustration, and overall becoming demotivated. However, I understood that as a leader and head of the department, I couldn't afford to "show weakness" or express dissatisfaction with the manager or the company in front of my subordinates! Every year, I celebrated achievements, nominated the best employees for bonuses and awards, and remained focused on achieving maximum results. Thanks to this, within three years our company increased its revenue almost fourfold and became the Ukrainian market leader in almost every product category we represented. Meanwhile I had the opportunity to move to another company for a higher position!

Components of Corporate Culture may include the following factors:

- **Language of Communication/ Communication Systems:** This includes the use of oral, written, and non-verbal communication, as well as gestures and facial expressions.

- **Awareness of One's Role in the Organization:** Some cultures favor concealing personal intentions, while others encourage their external expression. Some companies focus on collaboration, while others promote individual self-expression.

- **Appearance of Employees:** This involves neatness, the presence of special clothing or uniforms.

- **Adherence to the Daily Schedule:** Following the structured workday schedule.

- **Organization of Meals:** This refers to the duration and frequency of meals, whether there is one cafeteria for all employees or if it is divided between managerial and regular staff.

- **Relations within the Team and with Clients:** This includes interactions between individuals of different gender, age, religion, social status, and how conflicts are resolved.

- **Norms and Values of the Organization:** The foundational principles and ethical standards upheld within the company.

- **Motivation and Work Ethics:** Responsibility for the work performed, quality of work, evaluation of the work, and rewards, as well as opportunities for career advancement.

- **Belief:** Belief in success, help, support, justice, and personal abilities.

- **Organizational Symbols:** Rituals, slogans, organizational taboos, and other forms of symbolic representation.

Reflective task:

Are the values or norms of corporate culture formulated in your project? Based on the gathered information, invite key employees and together review and document the values and elements of the corporate culture.

KEY TAKEAWAYS FROM THE SEAT OF THE TABOURET: MISSION, VISION, VALUES

The Seat of the Tabouret is essential for uniting and holding its legs together. Among the key factors capable of bringing people together are **Mission, Vision, and Values**.

- **Mission** answers the question: "Why?" — thereby giving meaning to the organization's activities. The components of the Mission include an understanding of the target audience (who we are working for), the field of activity, and the broader impact of the organization's work.

- **Vision** answers the question: "Where?" — shaping the perspective of a "better future in Christ." The components of the Vision are the Goal, Strategy, and Plan.

- **Values** answer the question: "What is important to us?" — thus acting as the constitution or guiding principles of the organization. The collective set of values forms the Corporate Culture.

Reflective task:

- *Conduct a review of the materials in the section "The Seat: Mission, Vision, Values."*

- *Mark key points — Highlight, underline, or make notes in the margins of the parts you believe are worth sharing with your team.*

- *Plan your presentation — Decide where and how you will share these insights with your team.*

- *Assess the current state — Based on your understanding of the current situation in your project, evaluate the presence of a strong "Seat" in your project.*

- *Team discussion — Invite the relevant team members and discuss the goals and action plan for achieving them together.*

· Alex Marchuk ·

Final words

Better is the end of a thing than the beginning thereof: and the
patient in spirit is better than the proud in spirit.
— Ecclesiastes 7:8

I thank God for helping me complete my part — sharing the Tabouret Principle — to the very end. Now, the final step remains — you need to implement the Tabouret Principle in your projects!

From my side, I can tell you that this will be an exciting experience that will not only help your team unite and grow closer to one another but will also have a positive impact on the lives of many people around you!

I sincerely hope that the Tabouret Principle will help you and your project reach a level where, on one hand, you can already enjoy the fruits of your labor today, and on the other — create an effective tool for improving the world around you!

I wish you the best of luck and pray that our Almighty, Loving Heavenly Father will inspire and guide you on your journey!

Amen!

Bibliography:

1. Bible King James Translation

2. Merriam-Webster Dictionary

3. Hans Hamoen, Doing Business with God,

4. The Standish Group International, Inc., CHAOS Report (1994)

5. Ichak Kalderon Adizes, Managing Corporate Lifecycles, Book Club "Family Leisure Club", 2018

6. Masaaki Imai, Kaizen: The Key to Japan's Competitive Success, Alpina Publisher, 2018

7. Abraham Harold Maslow, Motivation and Personality, Piter, 2012

8. Frederick Herzberg, The Motivation to Work, Taylor & Francis, 1993

9. Alexander Osterwalder, Yves Pigneur, Business Model Generation: A Handbook for Visionaries, Game Changers, and Challengers, Nash Format, 2017

10. W. Chan Kim, Renée Mauborgne, Blue Ocean Strategy: How to Create Uncontested Market Space and Make the Competition Irrelevant, Book Club "Family Leisure Club", 2018

11. James Gilmore, Joseph Pine, The Experience Economy: Competing for Customer Time, Attention, and Money, Vivat, 2021

12. Viktor E. Frankl: Yes To Life In Spite of Everything, Rider & Co, 2021

13. Viktor E. Frankl: Man's Search For Ultimate Meaning, Ebury Press, 2011

14. Lee Kuan Yew: From Third World to First World The Singapore Story 1965-2000, KM-Books, 2016